READ-ALOUD PLAYS

Ancient World

by Alexandra Hanson-Harding

NEW YORK • TORONTO • LONDON • AUCKLAND • SYDNEY
MEXICO CITY • NEW DELHI • HONG KONG • BUENOS AIRES

Teaching *Resources*

This book is dedicated to Brian, Moses, and Jacob, with love.

With thanks to Sarah Glasscock and Mela Ottaiano for their contributions to this book.

Cover design by Maria Lilja
Cover illustration by Holly Jones
Interior design by Melinda Belter
Interior illustrations by Teresa Southwell, Mona Mark (page 4), Holly Jones (page 15), Greg Harris (page 62)

Copyright © 2005 by Alexandra Hanson-Harding. All rights reserved.

ISBN 0-439-22261-3

Printed in the U.S.A.

1 2 3 4 5 6 7 8 9 10   40   12 11 10 09 08 07 06 05

Contents

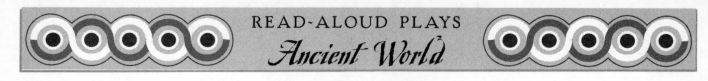
Introduction

History is made by powerful men and women who shape nations' destinies. But it is also made by the millions of people who live regular lives in the shadows of the famous. These ordinary citizens give a society continuity.

People back in ancient times lived lives much like ours—rich with humor, aggravation, tragedy, and joy. Their societies weren't perfect. They could be stifling or chaotic for the people who lived in them. People fell between the cracks or were forced to lead lives they didn't choose—just as many do today. Some of their customs seem strange, even barbaric, to us.

And yet the civilizations of the ancient world profoundly influenced the way we live now. In lands as diverse as China and Egypt, stable governments allowed people the safety to lead their lives in relative freedom. This allowed great civilizations to flower. These societies are gone now, but there are echoes of their thought in our justice system, our ways of organizing our government, our arts, and many other parts of life. In some ways, we are still citizens of that ancient world.

In the course of reading these plays, students will come to understand not only the individual cultures, but some of the forces that shape all civilizations, ancient and modern. Some of these forces include trade, self-defense, religion, government, the development of new technology, and family. Your students will be able to compare and contrast the gifts and problems of each of the eight societies profiled here. In doing so, they can enrich their understanding of history. Why does that matter? As historian Peter N. Stearns said, "Why study history? The answer is because we virtually must, to gain access to the laboratory of human experience."

Alexandra Hanson-Harding

HARSH JUSTICE

CAST OF CHARACTERS

GUBARRU, *a house-builder*

SHESHBAZZAR, *Gubarru's brother-in-law*

LADIES 1–4

BALASHI, *Gubarru's foreman*

INANNA, *a tavern keeper and Gubarru's wife*

AMURRU, *a neighbor*

TIAMAT, *Amurru's wife*

BEL-IBNI, *a neighbor* • **KUDDA,** *a scribe*

NARRATOR

SCENE ONE

NARRATOR: The year is 1760 B.C. in Babylon, during the reign of King Hammurabi. In a wealthy neighborhood, workers are busy building a three-story mud-brick house.

GUBARRU: Sheshbazzar!

(Ladies 1–3 walk by.)

SHESHBAZZAR: Hello, ladies. What a refreshing sight you are on a broiling hot day. Your loveliness is like a drink of cool water from the freshest spring.

LADY 1: What a creep! Ignore him.

LADY 2: We don't need trash talk from strangers.

LADY 3: His talk is like the sewage flowing into the Euphrates River.

(They laugh and walk off.)

GUBARRU: Sheshbazzar! Did you make sure to pack the mud tightly enough around that wooden roof beam? These cedar beams from the land of the Phoenicians cost a king's ransom. The family we're building this house for wants only the finest. We must make sure that our workmanship is also the highest quality.

(Lady 4 walks by.)

SHESHBAZZAR: Hello there, radiant one!

LADY 4: Mind your own business!

GUBARRU: Sheshbazzar! Please pay attention to your work. Did you do everything I asked? Did you mix the mud until it was smooth?

SHESHBAZZAR: Just because I'm your wife's little brother, you don't think I can do anything right.

GUBARRU *(sighing)*: Okay, okay!

SHESHBAZZAR: I feel *very* insulted. You should trust me.

(Gubarru walks away, shaking his head. He joins Balashi.)

BALASHI: How's it going, boss?

GUBARRU: Why must I have my lazy brother-in-law working for me? He does everything as slowly as possible.

BALASHI: He seems a little girl-crazy.

GUBARRU: If I give Sheshbazzar a simple task, like making mud bricks, he complains he's bored. He *can* do jobs that need skill, like working on the roof, but it's hard to get him to pay attention—

Read-Aloud Plays: Ancient World • Scholastic Teaching Resources

BALASHI: Especially if a female walks by. Isn't there anything you can do to get rid of him?

GUBARRU: You know my wife, Inanna. As far as she's concerned, her little brother can do no wrong.

BALASHI: Why don't you just tell her you're going to fire him and be done with it?

GUBARRU: I couldn't stand to upset her. Except for babying her brother, she's the most perfect woman who ever lived. I only hope Sheshbazzar did his work properly. It's impossible to check now that the mud's already dried.

SCENE TWO

NARRATOR: A few weeks later, Inanna is busy working at her outdoor beer stall in the neighborhood.

INANNA: Beer! Freshly brewed beer! Don't drink dirty water from the river! Drink my clean, refreshing beer and save yourself from disease!

(Balashi runs in.)

BALASHI: I have bad news, Inanna!

INANNA: Oh no! Is some evil woman chasing my precious brother? They think Sheshbazzar's irresistible.

BALASHI: Your husband has been arrested!

INANNA: Gubarru? Arrested? Why?

BALASHI: The house he was building fell down!

INANNA: Was anyone hurt?

BALASHI: The owner. If he dies they'll put your husband to death!

INANNA *(wailing)*: Oh, no! What should I do?

(Amurru, Tiamat, and Bel-ibni run in.)

AMURRU: What is it, neighbor?

INANNA: My husband has been arrested. The house he was building fell down and injured the owner.

TIAMAT: That sounds bad.

INANNA: Oh, why is this misfortune happening? I try to do my best. I wear lucky beads in my hair and amulets around my neck and arms. I went to the ziggurat to make a sacrifice to the Virgin Mother Ishtar. I pray to the all-powerful Lord God Marduk. And still, this misfortune plagues us! Oh, my poor Gubarru!

BEL-IBNI: Did you leave out some sacred ritual perhaps? Is that why the evil eye has come to your door?

INANNA: No, I—alas, I did! I should have made a clay image of the demon that is tormenting Gubarru.

BEL-IBNI: And then put it in a little boat, set it on the Tigris River, and said prayers until the boat capsized.

INANNA: Or sprinkled myself with holy water from the Euphrates. Or—

AMURRU: Maybe you should have given money to the priests of Marduk so they would pray for you.

BEL-IBNI: Do you think this could have anything to do with your brother?

INANNA: Why do you ask?

BEL-IBNI: The question just popped out.

INANNA: I know you think Sheshbazzar's difficult. Nobody understands him. He has a romantic soul, yet he's forced to work for a living.

TIAMAT: There's no use making Inanna feel bad. The demons that bring misery to our lives are powerful and sneaky. The only thing we can do is to go down to the king's stela at the temple of Marduk and see what the law says.

INANNA: None of us can read.

TIAMAT: We'll find someone who can. Come on!

AMURRU: My wife is right! Come on, everyone.

SCENE THREE

NARRATOR: Inanna and her neighbors travel to the temple of Marduk. Outside the gates, scribes sit in the shade, waiting for customers who want someone to write a letter or a legal document for them. Inside, rising eight feet into the air, is a shiny black stone stela covered with writing.

AMURRU: Look at the picture at the top. It shows our king, Hammurabi, standing before the sun god, Shamash. See, Shamash is giving Hammurabi the great laws.

TIAMAT: Thank you so much for sharing that, husband. Since you know everything, why don't you tell us what the laws are?

AMURRU: I don't know how to read. Why don't *you* read it?

BEL-IBNI: Look, here's Kudda, the scribe. Scribes can read!

KUDDA: Does someone need a scribe?

TIAMAT: Inanna here is in trouble. Her husband got arrested, and we want to know what's going to happen to him. Can you read the stela for us?

KUDDA: That'll cost you. There are more than four thousand lines with two hundred eighty-one laws on it.

TIAMAT: Just read what's going to happen to her husband. A house he built fell down and hurt the owner.

KUDDA: Hmmm. Let me see what I can find.

INANNA: What does it say, Kudda?

KUDDA: I'll be happy to tell you—for a small fee.

TIAMAT: Have pity on the poor woman.

KUDDA: Did I not spend my whole childhood in the Tablet House using my sharpened reed to mark wet clay tablets? Was I not always getting caned by the teachers while you all were running and playing? Do I not now sit by the gates every day in the sizzling sun, where it's hot enough to fry a frog, waiting for work? Okay, maybe I wasn't the most diligent student and I didn't get a good government job, but time is money.

INANNA: Please, help me!

KUDDA: It will cost you one shekel. And, say, don't you own a beer shop?

AMURRU: This is an emergency! Just read the stela.

KUDDA: My throat—too dry—

INANNA: All right! Tiamat, dear neighbor, will you bring the man some beer while I pay him?

(Tiamat leaves and then returns with a cup.)

KUDDA: Ahh! As we say, beer is "joy to the heart" and "happiness to the liver."

BEL-IBNI: Maybe if your liver wasn't so happy you'd be more successful.

KUDDA: Do you want me to read or don't you?

EVERYONE: Yes!

KUDDA: Ahem. "I am King Hammurabi . . . who conquered the four quarters of the world, who made great the name of Babylon, who made the heart of the god Marduk rejoice, who worships Marduk every day, who—"

BEL-IBNI: Are you reading the whole thing?

KUDDA: Isn't that what you want?

INANNA: Please tell me that my poor Gubarru won't be put to death. It would break my heart to think of him sent off to Aralu, the dark and shadowy afterworld, to live under the cruel rule of the god Nergal!

KUDDA: Here's something: "If anyone breaks a hole into a house to steal things, he shall be killed and buried in front of that hole."

INANNA: Gubarru is not a thief!

KUDDU: How about this one: "If a man wishes to separate from his wife, he shall give that wife her dowry. When she has brought up her children, she may then marry the man of her heart."

INANNA: I love my husband!

AMURRU: Keep reading, Kudda.

KUDDA: Okay, let's see. "If a son strikes his father, his hands shall be cut off." Nope, that's not it. "If a man puts out the eye of another man, his eye shall be put out."

AMURRU: A friend of mine is a doctor. He operated on this guy's eye, the operation didn't work, and the government cut off both his hands!

BEL-IBNI: What would have happened if he *had* succeeded?

KUDDA: Wait, I saw it here a minute ago—"If a doctor . . . saves an eye, he shall receive ten shekels in money."

TIAMAT: I had a friend whose slave ran away. It turned out that his neighbor hated him and was hiding the slave in his house!

BEL-IBNI: What did they do to the neighbor?

TIAMAT: They put him to death, of course! As the old saying goes, "In a city that has no watchdogs, the fox is the overseer."

INANNA: But what can *I* do to help Gubarru?

KUDDA: Inanna, if you have an extra shekel, I *might* be able to give you some advice.

INANNA: Here—anything to save my poor Gubarru!

KUDDU: First, make sacrifices to the gods so that the man who was hurt survives. But if he doesn't, this might help. Before your husband speaks in court, tell him this—

(Kuddu whispers into Inanna's ear.)

Read-Aloud Plays: Ancient World • Scholastic Teaching Resources

SCENE FOUR

NARRATOR: A few days later, Inanna visits her husband in jail.

INANNA: It's so sad to see you in this dark, dank prison.

GUBARRU: My darling, you're like sunlight itself. How I've missed you. When I see your face, I think of our wedding day. Remember when I poured oil on your head during the ceremony?

INANNA: I remember it well. I also remember how handsome you looked in your eye makeup with your freshly curled hair.

GUBARRU: What a sweet moment it was when I put the veil on your head and said, "I am your husband, and you are my wife, and like the fruit of a garden I will give you children." Inanna, we hardly knew each other then, but I knew I would love you forever!

(They look at each other and sigh.)

INANNA: What happened to make the house fall?

GUBARRU: My darling, I'm so ashamed of myself. I should have checked your—the workers—more closely. Your—a worker—didn't pack the mud tightly enough around a roof beam and it fell.

INANNA: It was my brother's fault, wasn't it?

GUBARRU: No, darling. It was my fault. I should have watched more carefully while the work was being done. I shall carry the shame of hurting the poor owner for the rest of my life. If he dies—

INANNA: Don't despair, husband. I've been praying to the gods. I've also been talking to some people, and this is what I learned. A person accused of a crime is allowed to throw himself into the Euphrates River. If the current brings him back to shore alive, then the gods have found him innocent.

GUBARRU: What if he drowns?

INANNA: You're a strong swimmer.

GUBARRU: Yes I am, thank Marduk!

INANNA: Then we must have faith. But, oh, Gubarru, I feel so awful about my brother! This is all his fault!

GUBARRU: No, Inanna. It's my fault. I should always double check—no, triple check—everything.

INANNA: I know Sheshbazzar can be a little difficult.

GUBARRU: Don't even mention it. I'm a very strong swimmer.

INANNA: I'd hate for you to take that risk. But I know Sheshbazzar would drown in two seconds.

SCENE FIVE

NARRATOR: A few weeks later, Inanna sweeps the front of her tavern. She sees a man walking up the street. Inanna runs to hug her husband.

INANNA: Gubarru! You're free!

GUBARRU: I missed you so much.

(Amurru, Tiamat, and Bel-ibni enter.)

TIAMAT: Gubarru's back!

AMURRU: What happened?

GUBARRU: The owner of the house recovered completely! We'll be paying for years to rebuild his house, but—

INANNA: —but we'll to do it together.

BEL-IBNI: Marduk be thanked! Welcome back, neighbor.

GUBARRU: Where's Sheshbazzar?

INANNA: Oh—he got another job. He's working for a merchant, traveling around the empire, selling pots. Of course, now even more women will bother him, but what can I do? I hope you're not too insulted that he left, husband.

TIAMAT: Too much family in business together is not always a good thing.

GUBARRU: I'll manage without Sheshbazzar somehow. Don't worry yourself.

Read-Aloud Plays: Ancient World • Scholastic Teaching Resources

Background on Babylonia

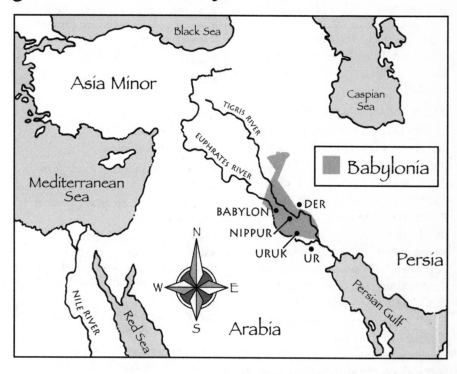

Two mighty rivers that flow southeast into the Persian Gulf have been the home to some of the world's earliest civilizations. The land where these cultures flowered was called Mesopotamia, which means "land between the rivers." One of these great civilizations was the Babylonian Empire.

Hammurabi's Laws

King Hammurabi (1728–1686 B.C.) was one of Babylonia's greatest leaders. He laid out 282 laws covering every area of life and had them carved into pillars of stone that were displayed in public places.

This code of laws wasn't the only code of its kind, but it's the earliest one we know of today. In the early 1900s, a stela containing Hammurabi's code was discovered in Mesopotamia in the ancient city Susa. The stela now stands in the Louvre Museum in Paris.

Hammurabi's laws give a detailed picture of the concerns of people in Babylonian society. Many of the laws are humane and just— including laws protecting the rights of women, children, and slaves, and those dealing with property disputes. Others are harsh and empha- sized what the Romans would later call *lex talionis*, the law of retalia- tion or "an eye for an eye."

Women's Role in Babylonia

The Babylonians had a relatively enlightened attitude toward women, although their status was not as high as it was in Egypt. Most tavern keepers were women, and women sometimes held other jobs, such as scribes. (The Babylonians drank a lot of beer—about 40 percent of their grain went into beer production.) Hammurabi's laws detail many of Babylonian women's rights and responsibilities.

Thinking and Discussing

WEDDING BELLS: What did stu- dents think of the description of weddings in this play? You might want to have them compare Babylonian weddings with those in other cultures by having them read the plays about China and Rome. How were the weddings different from each other in these three cul- tures? How are they different from weddings today?

CRUEL JUSTICE?: Do students believe that the punishments for crimes listed in the play were fair? If not, what kind of punishment would they have recommended? Discuss why we have codes of laws and what makes punishment effective.

LUCKY CHARMS: Inanna tries to ward off tragedy by wearing amulets and performing rituals to keep away the evil eye. What kind of supersti- tions do we have today? For instance, we're familiar with the notion that Friday the thirteenth, black cats crossing our paths, and breaking mirrors all cause bad luck. Athletes often have special socks or lucky coins they carry with them on game day. Why do students think that superstitions continue to have a role in our lives?

Researching and Doing

MAKE A ZIGGURAT: Have students research ziggurats, Babylonian tem- ples, and then make a model of a ziggurat out of different-sized boxes and other materials. In addition to

finding out why Babylonians and other Middle Eastern people constructed religious temples in this way, ask them to research what kind of features their houses of worship have. Why, for example, do many Christian churches have steeples?

BABYLONIAN FEAST: Babylonians traditionally served food on a tray placed on a low table. Their diet included the following foods: apples, dates, apricots, plums, pistachios, cucumbers, onions (which the Babylonians ate raw), millet, barley, lentils, cheese (especially goat or sheep cheese), and pita bread. Hold your own Babylonian feast. As students sample the food, ask if they think the Babylonians' diet was healthy or unhealthy. How does it compare to their own diets? Challenge students to do further research on the Babylonians' diet on the Internet or in the library.

LAW AND ORDER: Have groups of students look up Hammurabi's laws on the Internet (see www.yale.edu/lawweb/avalon/medieval/ham frame.htm). Ask them to select four

Vocabulary

amulet: a charm with symbolic magical powers meant to protect the wearer

cedar: an evergreen tree

dank: unpleasantly humid or damp

dowry: money or goods a wife brings to a marriage

rejoice: to feel joyful

ritual: an act used in a religious ceremony

scribe: a public secretary or clerk in ancient times

shekel: the smallest unit of Babylonian currency (Sixty shekels made up one mina. A shekel was made of and worth about half an ounce of silver.)

stela: a stone slab or pillar, usually carved or inscribed

ziggurat: a special kind of Babylonian temple built in the form of a stepped pyramid

or five laws and then defend them to the rest of the class. Then challenge the class to rewrite the laws they believe are unfair. Emphasize

the importance of the class's coming to a consensus. Extend the activity by having students look for newspaper and magazine articles about our criminal justice system. Are they convinced that the punishments they read about fit the crime? Have them defend their reasoning in an essay.

References

Brown, Dale M., ed. *Mesopotamia: The Mighty Kings.* New York: Time-Life Books, 1995.

*Contenau, Georges. *Everyday Life in Babylon and Assyria.* London: Edward Arnold, 1954.

Saggs, Henry W.F. *Babylonians.* Berkeley: University of California Press, 2000.

BOOKS FOR STUDENTS

Landau, Elaine. *The Babylonians.* Millbrook, NY: Millbrook Press, 1997.

Nardo, Don. *Empires of Mesopotamia.* San Diego: Lucent, 2000.

out of print

Egypt, 1250 B.C.

IN THE BEAUTIFUL HOUSE

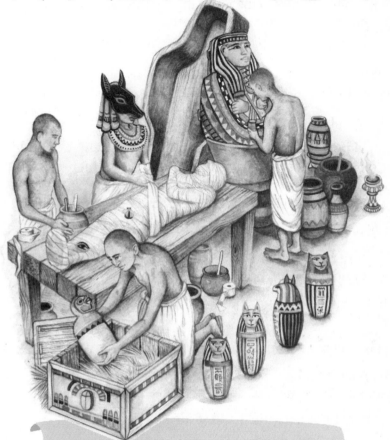

CAST OF CHARACTERS

TIY, *an Egyptian boy*

KIYA, *an Egyptian girl and Tiy's sister*

WENENKHU, *a priest and the father of Tiy and Kiya*

SENEBTISI, *the mother of Tiy and Kiya*

PAMIU, *a priest* • **TEPEMKAU,** *a priest*

WOSRET, *a priest* • **PTAHHOTEP,** *a priest*

SENBI, *a priest*

BODIES 1–4 *(nonspeaking roles)*

NARRATOR

SCENE ONE

NARRATOR: In 1250 B.C., during the time of King Ramses II, a family is having dinner at their home near Thebes. This is a calm and peaceful period in Egypt's three thousand-year empire.

TIY: Why do we have to live outside the gates of the city? The other kids treat us like we're weird.

KIYA: They're mean to us just because Papa takes care of the dead.

WENENKHU: It sounds like you're ashamed of what I do.

SENEBTISI: How dare you speak to your father that way, children! He has a very important job in the Beautiful House. What could be more valuable than a priest who helps the dead gain immortal life? What if he didn't have a job? You'd be living in a hut, eating boiled papyrus roots every day.

TIY: I'm sorry, Papa.

WENENKHU: Don't forget—when you're a little older, you'll be my apprentice. Then you'll learn to help the dead, too.

SENEBTISI: I have an idea! Why don't you take the children with you to work tomorrow?

WENENKHU: Take them to work? I'm not sure that's a very good—

SENEBTISI: The children might learn something useful, Wen, especially since they don't appreciate the work you do.

WENENKHU: I'm still not sure it's the best idea—

SENEBTISI: Nonsense!

WENENKHU: But Sen, I'm not sure Tiy's ready to see what I do yet.

SENEBTISI: Tiy'll be fine—and so will Kiya.

WENENKHU: All right, my beloved wife. Tomorrow I'll take you kids with me.

SENEBTISI: And you'd better behave yourselves!

SCENE TWO

NARRATOR: The next morning, the sun is shining bright and hot into the family's mud-brick home, as it does almost every day. Before breakfast, Tiy and Kiya are playing a board game called senet. A small monkey is perched on Tiy's shoulder.

SENEBTISI: Children, did you feed the sacred crocodile?

CHILDREN: Yes, Mother.

SENEBTISI: Then eat your bread and leeks. It's easy for you kids to get dressed. All you have to put on are your earrings. Your papa has to put on his linen skirt and jewelry and then make up his eyes.

TIY: Can the monkey come with us?

SENEBTISI: Absolutely not. *Achoo!*

KIYA: I'm sorry about your cold, Mother.

SENEBTISI: Thank you, dear. I'll say an incantation to get rid of it: Depart, cold, son of a cold, you who breaks the bones, destroys the skull and makes sick the seven openings of the head! *(She breathes in deeply.)* Ah, much better! Put away that game of senet, and eat your breakfast.

KIYA *(muttering)*: Spending the day with dead bodies. This is going to be *so* much fun.

SCENE THREE

NARRATOR: Wenenkhu, Kiya, and Tiy are crossing to the western bank of the Nile in a boat made of reeds. They see crocodiles floating like logs in the river. Big white and black birds called ibises flap overhead.

WENENKHU: Here's a test, children. Which god has the head of an ibis?

KIYA: Oh, oh, I know! Thoth!

WENENKHU: And who is Thoth?

TIY: He's the god of writing, and astronomy, and geometry, and medicine—

KIYA: —and talking, and writing, and he measures the earth, and he records all knowledge.

WENENKHU: Excellent!

TIY: Why is the Beautiful House on the other side of the river, Papa?

WENENKHU: Each day, the great sun god, Amun-Re, travels across the sky in his boat. He starts in the deserts of the east and passes over our holy river, the life-giving Nile. Then Amun-Re passes the black land—the rich soil along the riverbanks, brought to us by the yearly floods. Finally he passes into the red land of the western desert and disappears until another day. We bury the dead in the west because that's where the sun sets.

KIYA: Is that why we call the dead Westerners?

WENENKHU: That's right.

Read-Aloud Plays: Ancient World • Scholastic Teaching Resources

TIY: Why do we make mummies of the dead anyway?

WENENKHU: Do you remember the story of what happened to the great god Osiris?

KIYA: Osiris ruled the land of Egypt, and he was a good and wise ruler. Right?

WENENKHU: Very good, Kiya! Do you know what happened next, Tiy?

TIY: Osiris's evil brother Seth got hold of him. Seth ripped Osiris up and buried the pieces in fourteen different places.

KIYA: The goddess Isis, Osiris's wife and sister, found all the pieces. She put them together and breathed life back into him. Now Osiris is the king of the underworld.

TIY: But that doesn't explain why we make mummies.

WENENKHU: We hope to be restored, just as Osiris was restored. But, like Osiris, our bodies have to be restored, too. We used to bury our dead in the desert sands because the dry heat preserved their bodies for many generations. But they were often dug up and eaten by jackals. We had to find a way to take better care of the dead. Tiy, please—keep your hands in the boat. I don't want your fingers bitten off by a crocodile!

SCENE FOUR

NARRATOR: On the western side of the Nile, Wenenkhu, Tiy, and Kiya reach a low series of buildings. Outside, under an awning, the priests, Pamiu and Tepemkau, are washing a body on a table.

KIYA: What's that horrible smell, Papa?

TIY: Why are there so many flies buzzing around?

PAMIU: After a few minutes, you won't even notice the smell.

WENENKHU: Ah, Pamiu. This is my son, Tiy and my daughter, Kiya. Children, these are my fellow priests, Pamiu and Tepemkau.

TEPEMKAU: Nice to meet you!

PAMIU: Welcome to the Beautiful House.

TIY AND KIYA (together): Thank you.

WENENKHU: When we receive a body, we bring it to this area, which is called the Place of Purification. We wash the body with water from the Nile to make it clean and pure for the next stop. Follow me into the Beautiful House.

Read-Aloud Plays: Ancient World • Scholastic Teaching Resources

SCENE FIVE

NARRATOR: Wenenkhu leads Tiy and Kiya into the building. Bodies are laid out on tables. The priests, Wosret, Ptahhotep, and Senbi, are working on the bodies.

TIY: Papa, are those people on those tables dead?

WENENKHU: Of course, son.

KIYA: I think I'm going to be sick.

WENENKHU: Don't be frightened, children. You'll get used to it. Just stand back and stay out of the way of the priests.

KIYA: We'll stay *way* back. We promise!

TIY: Why is this place called the Beautiful House anyway? It's so hot and stinky—and *so* not beautiful.

WENENKHU: Because we make the dead beautiful for eternity. You'll see.

NARRATOR: Wosret puts a hook up a dead man's nose.

TIY: What is that priest *doing*?

WENENKHU: That's Wosret. He's pulling out the brain, sweetheart. If he left the brain in, it would rot the body. The brain isn't that important. Some say it makes the arms and legs move. But as far as I'm concerned, all the brain does is create nasty, drippy mucous.

TIY: Won't there be an empty hole in his head?

WENENKHU: He's a man of noble birth. Wosret will fill his head with resin.

NARRATOR: Ptahhotep pops out a dead woman's eyeballs with his thumbs.

KIYA: Why is he taking out that lady's eyes?

WENENKHU: Ptahhotep will replace them with pretty glass eyes. Now, watch what happens when Senbi cuts open the stomach of that body. We call Senbi "the Ripper."

NARRATOR: As Senbi makes the cut, Wosret and Ptahhotep throw stones at him.

WOSRET: Run away!

PTAHHOTEP: Depart, Ripper!

WOSRET: We command you to flee!

(Senbi runs away.)

KIYA: Why did they do that?

WENENKHU: Actually, I don't know why we do that. It's a ritual we perform as part of the cutting in. The meaning has been lost in the sands of time.

KIYA: No, Papa, why are they cutting that man open in the first place?

WENENKHU: When we get a body, we must act quickly before the decaying process sets in. We must take out the organs that rot.

TIY: What do you do with them?

KIYA: I don't think I want to hear this.

WENENKHU: See the four jars over there? Those are canopic jars. We preserve the organs we take out—liver and kidneys, intestines, stomach, and lungs—and then put them in the canopic jars. The heart is the only organ we preserve and put back into the body.

TIY: Why?

WENENKHU: The heart is a very important organ. It's the center of intelligence and the soul.

KIYA: Look at the lady on that table. She looks as if she could still be alive.

WENENKHU: Poor Hebeny! She was far too young to die. They tried every kind of medicine to cure her: lizard's blood, the teeth of a pig, rotten meat, the brains of a tortoise, an old scroll boiled in oil. Priests chanted for her and placed amulets around her neck. But, amazingly, nothing worked!

KIYA: She must have had an evil spell placed on her.

TIY: What are they doing to that man over there?

WENENKHU: We pack natron around the body. Natron is a special kind of salt that dries out the body.

KIYA: It's so much work.

WENENKHU: If we don't do it, how will the dead reunite with their bodies? When we die, all the different parts of us fly apart. You know what the *ba* is?

KIYA: It's the spirit that flies in our body like a bird in a cage when we're alive.

WENENKHU: And you know what our *ka* is?

TIY: The spirit that looks and moves just like us that is released after we die.

WENENKHU: And you know your shadow that follows you faithfully every day?

KIYA: Yes, Papa.

WENENKHU: Let me ask you then: What do you want to happen to you after you die? Don't you want to live with Osiris?

Read-Aloud Plays: Ancient World • Scholastic Teaching Resources

KIYA: Of course!

WENENKHU: You must be reunited after death with your *ba*, your *ka*, your shadow, and your body if you want eternal life.

TIY: Then it's not enough to be turned into a mummy.

KIYA: Being dead isn't easy.

WENENKHU: That's true. Before the dead can reach Osiris, they must say spells and answer many trick questions to get past the demons who guard the gates on the way. To help the dead, we wrap them up with the Book of the Dead.

TIY: What's that?

WENENKHU: It's like a handy test-taking guide that gives the dead many of the answers they'll need. If they pass these tests, they come to a river. Then the dead have to pass more tests before a ferryman agrees to take them across to the heart of the underworld.

KIYA: Do they get to live with Osiris then, Papa?

WENENKHU: First, the dead must pass the biggest exam of all. The jackal-headed god, Anubis, weighs their hearts against the Feather of Truth—which contains all of a person's evil deeds. The dead must make a confession before Osiris. They must confess all the bad things they *didn't* do, like—

(The priests step up and voice these confessions.)

WOSRET: I have not oppressed the poor.

PAMIU: I have not caused a slave to be ill-treated by his master.

TEPEMKAU: I have not starved any man. I have not caused any to weep. I have not assassinated any man.

SENBI: I have not committed treason.

PTAHHOTEP: I am pure.

TIY *(whispering)*: What if the dead person's heart and the feather don't balance?

WENENKHU: Those who fail the test are thrown to hungry, crocodile-like monsters that will keep devouring them forever. Those who pass can live with Osiris forever. They spend their days eating, drinking, playing senet, listening to beautiful flute music, and having fun in a land much like Egypt.

TIY: Now, that's more like it!

KIYA: Papa, is that man over there dried out enough to become a mummy?

WENENKHU: Almost.

KIYA: What happens when he's, uh, done?

WENENKHU: The drying takes about forty days. Then we put packing in the cheeks and arms to make them look fuller. We paint the women yellow and the men red and put henna on their hands and feet. Sometimes we put wigs on the dead or replace missing arms and legs. That way, they can go into the afterlife whole.

TIY: Then do you wrap them up?

WENENKHU: Yes, we wrap the body with many strips of fine linen to protect it for all eternity. Look over there. Do you see what Wosret is doing?

NARRATOR: Wosret is wrapping thin strips of cloth around a dead man's hand.

WENENKHU: First, Wosret wraps each finger and then the hand. Then he starts winding cloth around the head and around the rest of the body. It takes a lot of skill and a lot of cloth—more than four hundred fifty square yards of linen—to do it properly. Next we'll put the mummy in a coffin. The coffin will be placed in a tomb, which will have the person's name, and magical paintings to please the gods. We'll place the canopic jars in the tomb and other things to bring the person comfort in death. Cups, chairs, food—and *shabtis*, little figures of servants to help us in the next life.

TIY: I'd want to have plenty of figs in my tomb.

WENENKHU: The last step before we bury the dead is the Opening of the Mouth. We priests touch the mouth of the mummy and say special prayers. Otherwise the mummy won't be able to eat, drink, breathe, or talk. Then we put the mummy inside the tomb and seal it.

TIY: I still don't understand. Why is it so important to keep the body if the person has already passed the tests and is with Osiris?

WENENKHU: The Fields of Paradise are much like our Earth. It's possible we could die again.

KIYA: I used to think your job was sad, Papa, but I'm not so sure now.

WENENKHU: We do our best to take care of the dead. They may miss their families on earth—as we miss them—but they're having a good time in the afterlife.

TIY: Papa, what will happen when you die? Won't we ever see you again?

WENENKHU: I won't ever appear again on Earth. But if I'm good, I'll reach the Fields of Paradise. Someday you'll join your mother and me, and we'll all be together again.

KIYA: I'm going to hold my head up proudly from now on—no matter what anyone says about Papa's job.

TIY: I will, too. And I'll be proud to work in the Beautiful House some day.

Read-Aloud Plays: Ancient World • Scholastic Teaching Resources

Background on Ancient Egypt

For most of its history, Egypt was one of the most comfortable, serene, and secure places to live in the ancient world.

A Gift of the Nile

Egypt was a prosperous empire for 3,000 years, from about 3000 to 32 B.C., until the Romans turned it into a colony. Geography had a lot to do with Egypt's stability. "Egypt," wrote the ancient historian Herodotus, "is a gift of the Nile." Every spring, the Nile River would flood, leaving its banks covered with fertile soil. Bountiful crops allowed the Egyptians to amass great riches, while the desert that surrounded them helped protect them from invasion. Egyptians believed that their rulers were divine, that the weather and crops were a gift from the gods, and that they were the gods' grateful children.

Family Life in Egypt

Peasants and slaves lived hard lives in ancient Egypt. For many middle- and upper-class families, however, life was good, as we have learned from many ancient papyrus scrolls. Men and women wrote love poetry to each other, got married, and had large families. Women enjoyed more rights and respect than in most other ancient societies, and often ran their own businesses. They inherited property and passed it to their daughters. Children played with toys like marbles and dolls. Adults went to elegant parties where women wore waxy cones of perfume tied to their heads; the wax would slowly melt and scent their hair. Adults wore linen clothes, while children went naked. Both men and women wore make-up and were concerned about staying slim and healthy.

Religion in Egypt

The Egyptians had many gods. They believed that life first emerged from a marshy area much like the banks of the Nile. In parts of Egypt, crocodiles were considered sacred. Many families raised their own sacred crocodiles and decorated them with glass earrings. Egypt had a large priesthood and many magnificent temples were built to their gods. Most Egyptians were superstitious. They took magical cures for illnesses and recited incantations.

Egyptian Tombs and Mummies

The most famous tombs are the massive pyramids of the early kings of Egypt. But Queen Hatshepsut, Egypt's only female pharaoh, saw how eagerly grave robbers dug treasures out of the tombs and decided to have a magnificent tomb carved out of the hills west of the southern city of Thebes. Other pharaohs followed her example. Over time, hundreds of royals would be buried in this area, known as the Valley of the Kings. Among the pharaohs buried here are Ramses II, who ruled for more than 60 years, and the famous boy-king, Tutankhamen, whose treasure-filled tomb was found in the 1920s.

But Egypt's dead have not been allowed to rest in peace. In medieval times, Europeans believed that powdered mummy would cure their ailments. Traders dug up mummies by the thousands and sold them. Some Europeans were dosing themselves with powdered mummy until the mid-1800s. Tombs were also plundered for gold and other riches. Mummies were cut open by treasure hunters who hoped to find valuable amulets and other jewelry beneath the wrappings. Mummies also

became a curiosity. People would pay to see one unwrapped. In recent decades, however, the security of tombs has been preserved. Archaeologists work at burial sites under the supervision of Egypt's Board of Antiquities.

Thinking and Discussing

MUMMIES: Before students read the play, ask them what they know about mummies. From which sources have they gotten their information? What are their attitudes toward mummies? Do they find mummies frightening? Revisit the topic of mummies after reading the play. How have students' attitudes changed?

HOLY RIVER: Talk to students about how important the River Nile was, and is, to Egyptians because of its role in providing food and transportation. Ask students to find examples in the play of how the river influenced Egyptians in their religious and cultural ideas. Do they agree with Herodotus that "Egypt is the gift of the Nile"? How does geography affect the place where they live? What natural features are important to the location of your city or town?

THE LIFE BEYOND: Use this play as a springboard for a discussion of the afterlife. What do students think of the beliefs of ancient Egyptians about death? You may wish to let students compare their views of the afterlife with those of the ancient Egyptians. Are there common threads? Why would a culture spend time creating a belief system about what happens after death?

Researching and Doing

EGYPTIAN INVENTIONS: Divide your class into groups, and have them talk about Egyptian contributions to the following inventions:

Vocabulary

amulet: a charm with symbolic magical powers meant to protect the wearer

ba: the personality, which is represented as a tiny version of oneself

Book of the Dead: a guide for the dead, made up of prayers and spells

canopic jars: a set of four jars in which the Egyptians stored a mummy's preserved organs (liver and kidneys, intestines, stomach, and lungs)

henna: a reddish-brown dye made from the leaves of the henna plant

jackal: a doglike mammal

ka: the soul, which flies out at death, represented by a human-headed bird

incantation: a prayer

natron: a hydrated native sodium carbonate used in embalming in ancient times

senet: an ancient Egyptian board game

shabtis: small figurines representing servants and helpers who would care for the dead in the afterworld

the clock, geometry, ink, paper, the calendar, the census, the postal service, and so on. Set aside time for groups to present their findings. Encourage a wide variety of presentation forms, such as reports with graphics (diagrams, graphs, and illustrations), plays, and encyclopedia listings.

KNOW YOUR EGYPTIAN GODS: Ask students to find information about Egyptian gods and to make

trading cards based on their findings. They can include such categories as name, other names, appearance, and what each god does. Gods to focus on include Ra, Osiris, Isis, Hathor, Maat, Horus, Thoth, Anubis, Nut, Nephthis, Anubis, and Geb.

HIEROGLYPHICS: Explain that the Egyptians had two kinds of writing —the formal picture writing called hieroglyphics, and the more flowing hieratic for everyday use. More than 700 hieroglyphic symbols were in use at one time. Although many symbols represented whole words or concepts, some hieroglyphics represented single sounds. Challenge students to research hieroglyphics on the Internet (www.quizland.com/hiero.htm or www.pbs.org/wgbh/nova/pyramid/hieroglyph/) or in the library and then create their own hieroglyphic nameplates or calling cards.

References

*El Mahdy, Christine. *Mummies, Myth, and Magic in Ancient Egypt*. London: Thames & Hudson, 1991.

Wassynger, Ruth Akamine. *Ancient Egypt*. New York: Scholastic Professional Books, 1999.

BOOKS FOR STUDENTS

Scieszka, Jon. *Tut Tut*. New York: Puffin Books, 1998. (fiction)

Smith, Brenda. *Egypt of the Pharaohs*. San Diego: Lucent Books, 1996.

Tanaka, Shelley. *Secrets of the Mummies: Uncovering the Bodies of Ancient Egyptians*. New York: Hyperion, 1999.

Tyldesley, Joyce. *The Mummy*. London: Carlton Books LTD, 1999.

*out of print

Read-Aloud Plays: Ancient World • Scholastic Teaching Resources

Phoenicia, 700 B.C.

Masters of the Sea

CAST OF CHARACTERS

BELEAZAR, *a Phoenician trader*

HIRAM, *a shipowner-trader and Beleazar's father*

HANNIBAL, *Beleazar's uncle*

ASTAROTH, *Hannibal's wife and Beleazar's aunt*

DIDO, *Beleazar's wife*

SAILORS 1 and 2

AFRICAN TRADERS 1 and 2 *(nonspeaking roles)*

ALKMENE, *a Greek girl who becomes a slave*

GREEK GIRLS 1 and 2 *(nonspeaking roles)*

JEZEBEL, *Hiram's daughter*

ATALIA, *Beleazar and Jezebel's mother*

NARRATORS 1 and 2

SCENE ONE

NARRATOR 1: The year is 700 B.C. in the great city of Carthage on the coast of north Africa. Beleazar and his father Hiram are traveling around the Mediterranean Sea on a trading trip. They've stopped in Carthage to trade and to visit relatives.

NARRATOR 2: During the long visit, Beleazar has met—and fallen in love with—a young woman.

BELEAZAR: Father, I'd like your permission to marry Dido. You know she comes from a good family. They've lived next door to Hannibal and Astaroth for years. Doesn't Hannibal say how much he admires Dido's father? I know it's your choice whom I marry, but—oh, Father—I've never felt like this!

HANNIBAL: Dido's very smart. She'll make an excellent wife.

HIRAM: Wouldn't it be cruel to take Dido so far away from her family?

BELEAZAR: I want to stay in Carthage and work for Dido's father. He's exporting glass to Carthage's colonies along the African coast and in the Spanish islands. The business is doing well, and he could use my help.

HIRAM: But how could you stand to live here, son? The summer is so hot—especially when the huge sandstorms from the Sahara Desert darken the sky.

BELEAZAR: Carthage is new, Father! It's exciting!

HIRAM: What's your mother going to say? She won't like having her precious son so far away.

BELEAZAR: Dido and I could get married here. Then we can have a long visit at home in Tyre. Once Mother meets Dido, she'll be happy for me.

HIRAM *(to Astaroth)*: Your sister will be furious.

ASTAROTH: My sister may be mad at first. You know how much she loves a good wedding. But Atalia will approve of Dido.

HIRAM: I'm not afraid of my enemies—not even the Assyrians! But I'll be in trouble with my wife if Beleazar gets married here and not at home.

SCENE TWO

NARRATOR 1: A month later, Dido and Beleazar get married. A few days later, Hiram, Beleazar, and Dido sail west in a fleet of Phoenician ships.

NARRATOR 2: The ships hug the North African coast and sail past small trading posts.

DIDO: I love the salt air.

BELEAZAR: You're a true Phoenician. We're the masters of the sea!

Read-Aloud Plays: Ancient World • Scholastic Teaching Resources

DIDO: Why are we landing here? It looks like the middle of nowhere.

BELEAZAR: Wait and see.

HIRAM: Put out the trinkets!

NARRATOR 1: The two sailors row to shore. They arrange glass beads, tin bowls, cloth, and other goods on the beach. Then they row back to Hiram's ship.

DIDO: But there's no one around to trade with!

BELEAZAR: Just wait.

NARRATOR 2: African traders emerge from trees near the beach. The traders examine the goods and talk about them with each other. Then they disappear into the trees and return with chunks of gold, which they leave on the beach.

HIRAM (shaking his head): That's not enough gold!

NARRATOR 1: The African traders return with more gold and then disappear again.

HIRAM (nodding his head): Much better! Sailors, take the gold, and leave them the goods.

NARRATOR 2: The sailors row to shore and retrieve the gold. Then the African traders pick up their goods.

DIDO: The African traders could have just stolen the goods.

BELEAZAR: They knew if they did we'd never return. No more goods for them.

DIDO: They paid such a high price—

BELEAZAR: Don't feel sorry for them. They'll trade the stuff with their neighbors for even more gold. They'll make a profit just like we did. That's what trading is all about.

SCENE THREE

NARRATOR 1: Soon, most of the goods have been sold, and Hiram's ships are almost empty. They reach the Pillars of Hercules—the Strait of Gibraltar—where the Mediterranean ends and the Atlantic begins.

NARRATOR 2: Instead of turning northeast toward Phoenicia, they sail into the rough seas of the Atlantic.

DIDO: I love these wild seas!

BELEAZAR: You really are a true Phoenician.

HIRAM: That's good because we're on our way to the Tin Islands to fill our holds. We'll sell some of the tin on the way back, but we'll save most of it for our craftspeople in Tyre. They'll use the tin to make bowls and other things to sell.

DIDO: I've never heard of the Tin Islands.

BELEAZAR: I'll show you on the map. *(He points out the British Isles on a map.)*

HIRAM: Don't tell anybody, Dido. If the Greeks find out, they'll try to steal our business as they always do.

BELEAZAR: Sir, I think I saw something! Yes! Look—the sails of a Greek trireme!

HIRAM: Sailors, row to the east! Quickly!

BELEAZAR: We're losing them!

DIDO: Do you think the Greeks were following us?

BELEAZAR: Of course!

HIRAM: Once, a bunch of Greeks tried to follow a Phoenician ship to the Tin Islands. To stop them, the captain deliberately sank his own ship, even though it was full of cargo.

DIDO: What happened to him?

HIRAM: Our government repaid him. He was a true Phoenician hero!

SCENE FOUR

NARRATOR 1: After buying large supplies of tin, the Phoenicians sail south and enter the Mediterranean Sea through the Straits of Gibraltar. They stop at the city of Gadez (now Cádiz, Spain) to buy silver and wool to take back to Tyre. They trade along the southern coast of Europe, trying to avoid raids by Greeks.

NARRATOR 2: One day, they pass a small Greek island and see Alkmene and two other Greeks washing clothes on the beach. The Phoenicians quietly pull their boats into a nearby cove, sneak to the beach, capture the girls, and take them to the Phoenician ships.

ALKMENE: My father will pay you for my return.

HIRAM: If we go back to demand a ransom, the men of your village will attack us. Besides, you're worth more to me as a slave than as a hostage.

ALKMENE: A slave! You can't tell me what to do! I won't! I—

HIRAM: Beleazar, put her in the hold with the others until they calm down.

(Beleazar leads Alkmene away.)

DIDO: It breaks my heart to hear those girls cry.

HIRAM: You brought your own servant on the ship with you. She's not free, is she?

DIDO: No, but I treat her well. She isn't unhappy.

Read-Aloud Plays: Ancient World • Scholastic Teaching Resources

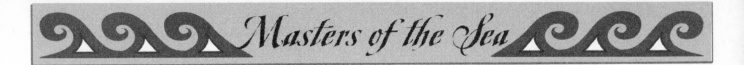

HIRAM: The Greeks would enslave us if they had the chance. They don't have rich land as the Egyptians do or forests of tall cedars as do we. They wouldn't have anything if they didn't steal it. It's only fair that we take what we can get, too.

DIDO (*under her breath*): Those poor girls!

<hr>

SCENE FIVE

NARRATOR 1: After sailing east and south, Hiram, Beleazar, and Dido finally reach the city of Tyre. Like most Phoenician cities, it's built on a peninsula.

NARRATOR 2: Tyre is far older than the city of Carthage, and shows its age.

HIRAM: At last we've arrived back in Tyre! There—see the light gleaming off the limestone temple of the god Melkart, and the city spreading below it?

BELEAZAR: It looks so crowded—especially after being on the open sea.

HIRAM: There's nowhere left to build on the peninsula. And we Phoenicians must live close to the sea. We ride in our ships the way others ride on horses and camels.

BELEAZAR: True, but Tyre still looks crowded.

HIRAM: Nonsense! Look at the fine harbor we've built. It's almost impossible for foreigners to invade us.

DIDO: What's that odor?

BELEAZAR: That fearsome stink comes from the dye-makers and their rotting shellfish.

HIRAM: You don't like the odor, but you like the prices our dyed cloth earns. Thanks to our dye, purple has become the color of royalty all over the world. Kings and noblemen across the Mediterranean pay us whatever we demand for our beautiful cloth. And the dye lasts forever.

BELEAZAR: The cloth brings in money, but the dye still stinks!

(*Atalia and Jezebel enter.*)

ATALIA: Why all the complaints, Beleazar? You've never talked like this about your home.

HIRAM: Look who's come down to the dock to meet us! My favorite daughter has come to welcome her father and brother home!

JEZEBEL: I missed you, Father!

ATALIA: Hello, husband.

HIRAM: And here's my beautiful wife.

(*The family hugs.*)

HIRAM: We have someone we'd like you to meet.

BELEAZAR: Mother, this is my wife, Dido. She comes from Carthage.

ATALIA: Wife?! You got married? And nobody asked my opinion?

DIDO: Hello, Mother-in-law. I've heard such wonderful things about you. I've been looking forward to this day for so long.

(She gives Atalia a big hug.)

ATALIA: Well, hello! Hiram, Beleazar—we'll have to talk about this.

HIRAM: There's plenty of time for that later. We've been apart for too long. Let's go home and celebrate.

SCENE SIX

NARRATOR 1: Later that evening, the family gathers for dinner.

HIRAM: It's wonderful to be back home. At sea, I longed to see Tyre's little streets, with their tall apartment buildings. But most of all, I missed you! Atalia, here's a little something for you.

ATALIA: What's this? Some kind of egg? It's gigantic!

HIRAM: It's an ostrich egg from Africa.

ATALIA: How unusual! I love the exotic things you bring home from your travels.

JEZEBEL: Remember Phelles, the monkey Papa brought home from Egypt? I loved that monkey.

HIRAM: I have another surprise for you, Atalia: a young Greek slave to fix your lovely hair. Come here, girl, and say hello to your mistress.

(Alkmene enters.)

ALKMENE *(sullenly)*: Hello.

HIRAM: Now go back to the kitchen.

(Alkmene leaves.)

ATALIA: She'll settle down soon enough. Tell me, husband, did you enjoy your adventures?

HIRAM: They reminded me that we Phoenicians truly are the most incredible people in the world.

ATALIA: Yes, dear. You always say that when you come home.

Read-Aloud Plays: Ancient World • Scholastic Teaching Resources

HIRAM: But it's true! Phoenicians own the sea. No one else knows how to sail at night or how to sail so far from land. Weren't we the first to light flares to guide our ships into harbor on stormy nights? No one builds ships the way we do or sails them as far. Who else dares to leave the Mediterranean and sail around Africa?

ATALIA: Yes, dear. Tell me, how was Carthage?

BELEAZAR: Wonderful! It's exciting and—there's something we have to tell you. Dido and I are moving to Carthage.

ATALIA: This is too much! First you get married, and now this! Won't you miss us?

JEZEBEL: Carthage is thousands of miles away!

BELEAZAR: I don't want to upset you, but I love Dido. I want to live in Carthage with her. Please try to understand.

ATALIA: I made a promise to myself when you were a baby, Beleazar. At the time, Phoenicia was having troubles with the Assyrians, and I was afraid you'd be selected as a sacrifice for Melkart. Hiram, do you remember? The mothers stood with empty arms as the priests threw their babies into the flames. How the mothers struggled not to cry. They knew tears would displease Melkart and make the gift of their children's roasted flesh less precious to him! I promised then that I wouldn't deny you anything you ever wanted.

BELEAZAR: Thank you, Mother. And believe me, I'm happy I didn't get thrown in the flames, too—and that I have you for a mother.

DIDO: I'm thankful, too, Mother-in-law. One thing I've learned over these months of traveling is the beauty of being a Phoenician. We of all peoples live lightly on the sea. We can easily sail to you, or you to us, whenever we like. I would love to visit Tyre again—with our baby.

JEZEBEL: I'm going to be an aunt!

DIDO: If it's a girl, we'll name her Atalia.

ATALIA: A grandchild! Maybe Jezebel and I will join Hiram on his next trip to Carthage. Come here, Daughter-in-law, and give me a hug.

Background on Phoenicia

The Phoenicians, also known as the Canaanites, arrived in what is now Lebanon by about 3000 B.C. Although no one knows exactly where they came from originally, experts believe it may have been the Persian Gulf region. It is thought that the Greeks tagged them as Phoenicians since they used the shellfish phoinikies to make purple dye. By 2600 B.C., Phoenicians were trading with the Egyptians, who later gained control over the Phoenicians until about 1400 B.C. Phoenicia soon became independent, and from 1200 B.C. began to flourish. They traded the large, beautiful cedar trees—a valuable commodity in the mostly dry Middle East—from the mountains. Then they began manufacturing lighter finished goods such as glassware, dyed cloth, and tin platters, which brought high profits. The Phoenicians also traded in slaves and other goods. Thanks to Phoenicians' prowess in sailing and trading, their trading posts extended around the Mediterranean. Successful in business, they ran their government not so much as a monarchy but as a coalition of business interests.

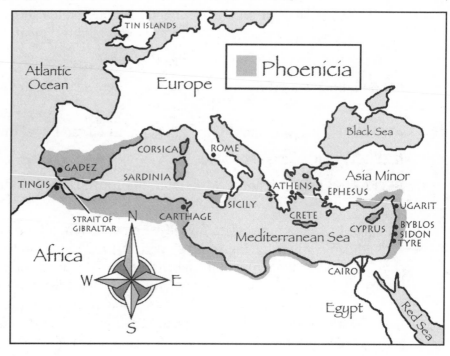

Phoenician History

Although the Phoenicians developed the first true alphabet, and their city of Byblos gave its name to the document we call the Bible, few Phoenician writings have survived. The papyrus they wrote on has disintegrated over time and their enemies also obliterated records. What little we know about the Phoenicians comes from other parts of the ancient world—from Greek and Hebrew writings. Homer mentions the fine glasswork of the Phoenicians. The Phoenician language died out after Tyre was conquered and then rebuilt by the Romans.

Phoenician Religion

Like other ancient cultures, the Phoenicians worshipped many gods, some which resembled the gods of their neighbors. They appeared to have practiced human sacrifice. In Carthage and in other parts of the former Phoenician empire, archaeologists have discovered altars where hundreds of human babies were sacrificed to the god Melkart in times of trouble.

The Decline of the Phoenicians

The Phoenician empire flourished for hundreds of years. But eventually, stresses led to its decline. As Greece became more and more powerful, it began to set up colonies that competed with Phoenician colonies for business. The Phoenicians were also weakened by the huge tribute they had to pay first to the Assyrians, and later to the Babylonians and the Persians. In 332 B.C., Alexander the Great destroyed the city of Tyre and forced its citizens into slavery. The city was later rebuilt by the Romans; one of its emperors, Septimus Severinus, was of Phoenician birth.

Carthage flourished long after Tyre was conquered. The Carthaginians were the largest power in the western part of the Mediterranean when the Romans began to expand their empire. One Roman senator ended every speech with the words, "Carthage must be destroyed!" The Romans and Carthaginians fought a series of wars, the Punic wars, which the Romans finally won.

Read-Aloud Plays: Ancient World • Scholastic Teaching Resources

Thinking and Discussing

BARTERING: Bartering, exchanging goods, and bargaining were important aspects of Phoenician business. Talk about the scene at the beach where Hiram and the African traders bargained with each other. Do they think that was a fair trade? Why was it so important for the Africans to keep trading with the Phoenicians? Then ask students whether they barter and bargain— for instance, do they barter their lunches? What other examples of bartering and bargaining do they see in their daily lives?

LEAVING HOME: Compare and contrast the situations of Dido and Alkmene. Both left their homes and traveled on Phoenician ships to Tyre. Ask students to think about and predict what happened to each woman after the play ended. Was Hiram justified in believing that the Phoenicians had to take what they wanted because the Greeks would do the same?

MAPPING THE JOURNEY: Display a world map, and call on volunteers to locate the Mediterranean Sea, the Straits of Gibraltar, Cádiz in Spain, the North African coast, and the British Isles. Point out where Tyre and Carthage were located. Then, based on the details in the play, have students discuss and chart the Phoenician ships' journey from Tyre to Carthage, North Africa, the Tin Islands, and back to Tyre.

Vocabulary

cedar: an evergreen tree

exotic: different or unusual

hostage: someone held against his or her will

limestone: a soft stone

Melkart: chief god of the Phoenicians

peninsula: land that extends into a body of water

ransom: payment made to free someone from captivity

trinket: a small ornament or object

trireme: an ancient ship with three banks of oars on each side

Researching and Doing

FIND THE NORTH STAR: The North Star was called the Phoenician star by the Greeks because the Phoenicians used it as a tool for navigation. Teach your students how to find the North Star in the night sky. Look at a star chart. Use a pin to poke holes in the bottom of a paper cup in the shape of the Big Dipper. Put a flashlight inside the cup. Then turn off the lights, and display the constellation on the ceiling. Let individuals or pairs make and present their own constellation cups.

SALE!: The Phoenicians were master salesmen. Pretend the Phoenicians are coming to town. Have students make advertising posters to entice local people to the market when the Phoenicians arrive. Encourage them to illustrate the posters with some of the wares the Phoenicians might bring and to describe why the wares are so tempting.

PUNIC WARS: In time, Carthage became more powerful than Phoenicia —so powerful that it challenged the Roman empire for dominance in world trade. This led to the Punic Wars. Ask groups of students to research the wars; they may give an overview or choose to focus on specific battles or leaders such as Hannibal, who led his troops across the Alps.

References

*De Camp, L. Sprague. *Great Cities of the Ancient World.* Garden City, NY: Doubleday and Company, Inc., 1972.

*Herm, Gerhard. *The Phoenicians: The Purple Empire of the Ancient World.* New York: William Morrow and Company, Inc., 1975.

*Herman, Zvi. *People, Seas, and Ships.* New York: G.P. Putnam's Sons, 1966.

*Moscati, Sabatino. *The World of the Phoenicians.* New York: Praeger History of Civilization, Frederick A. Praeger, Publishers, 1965.

BOOKS FOR STUDENTS

Fine, Jil. *Writing in Ancient Phoenicia.* New York: PowerKids Press, 2003.

Henty, G.A. *The Young Carthaginians.* Fort Collins, CO: Lost Classics Books, 2001.

*out of print

Assyria, 665 B.C.

THE OLD SOLDIER

CAST OF CHARACTERS

SHAMSHI-ADAD, *father of the family*

WARAD, *Shamshi-Adad's second son*

NISHI, *Shamshi-Adad's daughter*

ASHUR-DAN, *a scribe school student
and friend of Warad*

YASMAKH, *a warrior and uncle
of Warad, Nishi, and Tarim*

ZUKUTU, *Shamshi-Adad's wife*

TARIM, *Shamshi-Adad's first son*

NARRATORS 1–3

SCENE ONE

NARRATOR 1: It's 665 B.C. in Ninevah, Assyria (which is now northern Iraq). The Assyrian empire is one of the greatest empires the world has ever known, but it's also one of the cruelest. The empire is known for the harsh treatment of the peoples it conquers. Whole populations of defeated people are moved into different parts of the Assyrian empire, or—

NARRATOR 2: Enough! This play is about a nice Assyrian family. Shamshi-Adad looks at horses in the marketplace with his son, Warad, and his daughter, Nishi.

SHAMSHI-ADAD: Look at these fine horses from the Caucasus! It's wonderful how plunder has enriched our land.

WARAD (*under his breath*): Plunder. Slaves. Horses. Wars. That's all he thinks about.

NISHI: Shhhh, brother!

SHAMSHI-ADAD: Someday soon, Warad, you'll be charging into battle like your uncle Yasmakh. You'd look fine on this white stallion, with your sword gleaming.

WARAD (*yawning*): Whatever you say, Father.

SHAMSHI-ADAD: Do you know how much our way of fighting on horseback has changed over the years? Long ago, our archers had to climb off their horses to shoot arrows at the enemy.

(*Warad sneaks away while his father is talking. Nishi tries to wave him back.*)

SHAMSHI-ADAD: A little later, two archers would ride together. One held the reins, while the other shot arrows. Now we've trained our archers to shoot from the backs of moving horses. Isn't that fascinating, Warad? Warad?

(*Shamshi-Adad looks around in irritation.*)

NISHI: I love horses, Father. Let's keep looking.

SHAMSHI-ADAD: Where did that boy go?

NISHI: He *might* have gone to school to see if his clay tablets are dry.

SHAMSHI-ADAD: On his day off, your brother goes to school. If Warad didn't want to see horses, he could have been practicing swordplay with Ashur-Dan. Warad seems to have no interest in serving his country.

SCENE TWO

NARRATOR 3: A few days later, Warad is at scribe school. He and his friend and classmate, Ashur-Dan, are writing on clay tablets.

ASHUR-DAN: My writing looks crooked compared to yours, Warad.

Read-Aloud Plays: Ancient World • Scholastic Teaching Resources

WARAD: Your lines do look a little off. Press your stick into the wet clay like this. You'll get straighter lines that way.

ASHUR-DAN: Hey, that works! You must practice all the time.

WARAD: I practice so much I feel as if I'm practicing in my dreams.

ASHUR-DAN: I wish I wanted to be a scribe as much as you do. I don't want to spend my days writing up accounts of how big the barley harvest was. I want to be a soldier. But my father wants me to keep the accounts for his business.

WARAD: It's too bad my dad doesn't have you for a son!

(Nishi comes to the doorway of the school.)

NISHI: Warad! Guess what?

WARAD: Nishi! Girls aren't supposed to be here.

ASHUR-DAN: Don't be silly. Your sister is welcome any time!

NISHI: Oh! Ashur-Dan, I didn't know you'd be here.

WARAD: I'll bet. What do you want, sister?

NISHI: Good news! Uncle Yasmakh is here for a long visit! He's coming over for dinner tonight. Don't get lost in your work and forget to come home.

WARAD: Uncle Yasmakh! Cool!

ASHUR-DAN: Is this the soldier uncle you've been telling me about? Would you have room at the table for one more?

NISHI: You're always welcome at our house, Ashur-Dan.

WARAD: We'll be home in time. Now leave quickly before a teacher sees you!

(Nishi leaves.)

ASHUR-DAN: What a day! I'll get to meet your uncle *and* see your sister.

SCENE THREE

NARRATOR 1: That afternoon, Nishi and Uncle Yasmakh go for a walk. They visit the stela of battle scenes in the center of the city.

YASMAKH: The Assyrian army was the first to use iron armor and weapons. We were also the first to divide our units up into different specialties.

NISHI *(not really paying attention)***:** Really?

YASMAKH: Some units build roads so our soldiers can march thirty miles a day. Engineering units build catapults, and—Nishi, you usually love hearing about the army. What's wrong?

Read-Aloud Plays: Ancient World • Scholastic Teaching Resources

NISHI: Father and Warad keep fighting because Warad wants to be a scribe.

YASMAKH: Your father has always dreamed of Warad becoming a soldier.

NISHI: Let me ask you a question, Uncle. What qualities should a good soldier have?

YASMAKH: Good horsemanship, sword craft, the ability to fight fearlessly, the ability to follow orders and withstand hardships—

NISHI: Does Warad possess any of those qualities?

YASMAKH: He's dreamy, and the dreamy ones don't last a day. But he's still young. He can change.

NISHI: You have to help Warad, Uncle.

YASMAKH: What can I do?

NISHI: Talk to him—or them—or something. This is making everyone very unhappy.

YASMAKH: I'll do my best, Nishi. Besides, I have an announcement to make to the family, too.

SCENE FOUR

NARRATOR 2: Zukutu visits her husband and oldest son, Tarim, at the family tin shop.

ZUKUTU: Hello! I brought you all some freshly roasted locusts.

SHAMSHI-ADAD: Tarim, come have some fresh locusts.

TARIM: Thank you, Mother. If you don't mind, I must talk to some customers about our new tin bowls. We're trying a different design, which I think will sell well.

ZUKUTU: You're such a good boy, Tarim.

(Tarim leaves. He limps.)

ZUKUTU: Why do you look so troubled? Isn't business going well?

SHAMSHI-ADAD: Business is fine. And Tarim has learned everything about managing the shop. He's better at it than I am. He was born to be in the tin business.

ZUKUTU: Is that what's bothering you?

SHAMSHI-ADAD: No, I'm proud of Tarim. It's Warad. I thought he would become a warrior.

ZUKUTU: Do you regret letting him go to scribe school?

SHAMSHI-ADAD: It was a good idea at the time. Tarim was sick with the fever that made him lame. We were afraid he would die. And that would have left Warad to look after the business. We had to send Warad to school to prepare him.

ZUKUTU: Thankfully, Tarim recovered. Now we have two educated sons.

SHAMSHI-ADAD: Tarim will have the business. What does that leave for Warad?

ZUKUTU: Are you sure it's Warad's future that's troubling you?

SHAMSHI-ADAD: All right! I'm ashamed that he doesn't love his country enough to serve it. A few hundred years ago, we were almost wiped out! The people who live in the mountains, the deserts, and on the steppes envy us. They want to take our trade routes and our good land. It's a glorious thing to fight for this country! I would have—but I had to take over the business from my father.

ZUKUTU: You would have made a great warrior, Shamshi.

SHAMSHI-ADAD: That boy irritates me with his talk of becoming a scribe.

ZUKUTU: Tonight Yasmakh will be at dinner. Maybe his stories of glorious battles will change our son's mind. Perhaps Warad will decide to make history instead of recording it.

SCENE FIVE

NARRATOR 3: That night, the family is gathered around the dinner table.

YASMAKH: I haven't had such good food in a long time. Everything was delicious, Zukutu, from the fresh Tigris River fish to the goat cheese sprinkled on lentils.

(Ashur-Dan enters.)

ASHUR-DAN: I'm sorry I'm late. I got trapped behind a long column of slaves being taken to market. It took forever to get here.

SHAMSHI-ADAD: You're always welcome, Ashur-Dan. Maybe you can toughen up this soft son of mine with your swordplay!

ZUKUTU: Not now, Shamshi-Adad. Ashur-Dan, why don't you sit next to Nishi?

WARAD: After all, she saved the place for you.

NISHI: I did not!

ZUKUTU: Yasmakh, tell us about your latest adventures.

YASMAKH: Well, my unit reached a raging river that we had to cross, but the enemy burned all our boats. Our general ordered us to blow up the bladders of pigs until they were full of air. We floated across the river on the bladders. Then we attacked and defeated the enemy.

TARIM: Tell us again about the time you fought the Egyptians—how we Assyrians had iron swords, but the Egyptians only had bronze swords. So they quickly fled.

SHAMSHI-ADAD: Or the time you catapulted burning garbage over the walls to set cities on fire!

YASMAKH *(laughing)*: You just told the stories for me.

NISHI: As you can see, Ashur-Dan, we're very proud of Uncle Yasmakh.

ASHUR-DAN: Sir, I know soldiers travel a lot. I'd love to know where you've been.

YASMAKH: I was with King Sennacherib when he destroyed the holy city of Babylon and overran Judah and Israel. Under King Essarhaddon, I helped crush the rebellion in the Phoenician city of Sidon. Then I went to Egypt, where we forced the Pharaoh into exile. I've had a long career and seen many things . . . but now I have an announcement to make.

ZUKUTU: What is it, Yasmakh?

YASMAKH: I'm retiring from the army.

SHAMSHI-ADAD: You're *what!* Why?

YASMAKH: I'm taking the treasures I won from all these battles and buying a horse ranch.

SHAMSHI-ADAD: You're *what?* Why?

YASMAKH: I was a cavalry officer. I know what an Assyrian fighting man needs in a horse. I'm going to raise and train horses for the army.

SHAMSHI-ADAD: Forgive me, Yasmakh. After your glorious career, owning a horse farm seems so boring.

YASMAKH: I don't regret the years I spent in the army. But I've had enough.

ASHUR-DAN: Why is that, sir?

YASMAKH: It's not all parades and plunder, young man. Soldiers face many hardships —long marches, endless pots of burnt barley porridge, lack of freedom. Worst of all, I've seen so many brave young soldiers die. After a while, one doesn't want to make friends. One will only lose them.

SHAMSHI-ADAD: Yasmakh! How can you talk this way?

YASMAKH: I've seen rivers of blood and many beautiful cities in flame. We don't merely kill our enemies, we torture them. We cut off their skin and hang it on a wall to dry, put out their eyes, and *then* kill them. All this death wears out the soul.

SHAMSHI-ADAD: I can't believe I'm hearing such soft talk from you!

YASMAKH: Every time an Assyrian king dies, there are revolts against our rule. We're too harsh and greedy. Someday, a people will rise up and grind our cities into dust. They'll show us as little mercy as we've shown others. And it will serve us right.

Read-Aloud Plays: Ancient World • Scholastic Teaching Resources

SHAMSHI-ADAD: But fighting is how a man serves Assyria. And no matter what, the Assyrian Empire is the mightiest empire in the world! I don't understand why my foolish son doesn't love Assyria the way I do.

WARAD: I do love it. Look at our culture. Look at our beautiful city—the blue-enameled brick lion's gate and the "Palace Without Compare" on the Tigris with its sculptures of gods and hunting. Look at our art. Aren't these things more important than our ability to destroy?

SHAMSHI-ADAD: I suppose you have a point. But how are you going to make a living, Warad? The tin shop won't support you and your brother. And you can't support yourself by appreciating art.

WARAD: I have an announcement to make, too. King Ashurbanipal is collecting tablets about—well, everything!—for a library here in Nineveh. It will be one of the greatest libraries in the world. I've been offered a position there, copying tablets: ancient stories; recipes; information about medicines, laws, and how stars move in the sky; and facts about plants, animals, and different kinds of rocks from every part of the empire. Oh, Father, it will be wonderful to have so much knowledge gathered in one place! Preserving that information is my way of serving my country. If you'd give me permission, Father, I'd be the happiest son alive!

ZUKUTU: He does have to make a living, Shamshi.

YASMAKH: Warad has a hunger to learn. Let him be a scribe.

SHAMSHI-ADAD: Very well. I give you my blessing, son.

ASHUR-DAN: I have a surprise as well. My father's going to let me join the army after all. My little brother's going to scribe school in my place.

NISHI: That's wonderful, Ashur-Dan! Your dream will come true after all.

ASHUR-DAN: That's not my only dream. I would like to ask permission to marry Nishi. Then you would have a soldier in the family after all.

SHAMSHI-ADAD: All these changes! Let's celebrate with a toast.

(Everyone holds up a glass.)

SHAMSHI-ADAD: May our empire last forever!

EVERYONE: May our empire last forever!

NARRATOR 1: The Assyrian empire didn't last forever. Its time was almost at an end. In a little over fifty years, by 609 B.C., Assyria was conquered. The Chaldeans, Medes, and Babylonians not only leveled Nineveh, but they also marched the surviving Assyrians into slavery.

Background on Assyria

The Assyrians lived in the hilly country north of Babylonia, in present-day northern Iraq and southern Turkey. Assyria began to rise as a civilization around 1500 B.C. Few written records exist until the reign of King Shalmanesar I (1274–1245 B.C.), a cruel leader who blinded 14,000 enemy soldiers in one eye before selling them into slavery. That pattern of cruelty would continue throughout Assyria's history.

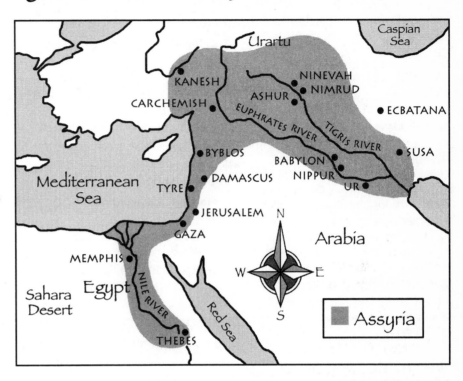

The Assyrians first reached the Mediterranean around 1100 B.C., under King Tiglashpilesar I. They continued to conquer other lands, exacting tributes of land, slaves, and treasure from those they vanquished and ruled by terror. Although mass revolts broke out whenever an Assyrian king died, their military grip was strong and most rebellions were put down. Among their techniques for controlling conquered populations was forcing huge numbers of people to move to a completely different part of the empire. As a result, the people became demoralized and disassociated from their homelands.

At the height of its empire (between 750 and 650 B.C.), Assyria extended from the Persian Gulf to the Mediterranean Sea, and, for a time, included Egypt. The empire eventually collapsed. The Assyrians were so hated that their enemies completely destroyed their beautiful cities.

Assyrian Civilization

In many ways, Assyrians were very sophisticated and advanced. They made formidable enemies not only because of their skill at fighting but also because of their skill at organization—from their armies to their government systems that provided strong, central rule. One of the Assyrians' greatest accomplishments was the building of a great library. This treasure house of knowledge contained everything from recipes to great philosophical ideas, like libraries today.

Assyrian Religion

The Assyrians borrowed many of their gods from their neighbors, the Babylonians—as they also borrowed the Babylonian dialect for writing literature. Their chief god was the fierce Assur, from whom they got their name. Assyrians believed that demons were everywhere, ready to bring evil or disease to whomever they touched. Incantations, charms, and priestly magic cures were used to try to defeat these demons.

Thinking and Discussing

CHOOSING CAREERS: All the male characters, except Tarim, have conflicts about the careers that have been chosen for them. Focus on the individual conflicts, and then discuss which characters got a chance to pursue their own dreams. What do these conflicts reveal about the Assyrians' way of life? With which character do students most identify, and why?

TWO SIDES OF THE ASSYRIANS: The Assyrians were among the most bloodthirsty people of the ancient world. They were also among the most cultured and artistic. Shamshi-Adad and his family don't seem cruel, although Uncle Yasmakh has witnessed cruelty in battle and participated in it, too. Ashur-Dan is eager to become a soldier, while

Read-Aloud Plays: Ancient World • Scholastic Teaching Resources

Warad wants to learn. How can a civilization be so cruel and so cultivated at the same time? How do the characters in the play help deepen students' understanding of this question?

LIBRARY: King Ashurbanipal collected more than 20,000 clay tablets in his library at Ninevah. He personally selected, and sometimes censored, each work. A warning in the library reads: *May all these gods curse anyone who breaks, defaces, or removes this tablet with a curse which cannot be relieved, terrible and merciless as long as he lives. . . .* Discuss whether librarians should have the right to censor material in a library. Also ask students to suggest three or four titles that any library should have and to talk about the role that libraries play in their everyday lives.

Researching and Doing

REMEMBERING WAR: Contact a local VFW and ask if any veterans would be willing to share their war experiences with student interviewers. Before the interviews, brainstorm a list of questions, such as the following: *Which war did you fight in? How did you become a soldier? What were the best and worst aspects of your wartime experiences? How did your view of being a soldier change after you fought in your battle?* After the interviews, set

---

Vocabulary

cavalry: units of soldiers who fight on horseback

catapult: a huge machine that hurls rocks or other dangerous objects into enemy territory

exile: a forced removal from a person's native land

locusts: grasshopper-like insects

loot: something taken by force

scribe: a public secretary or clerk in ancient times

stallion: a male horse used for breeding

stela: a stone pillar or slab, usually carved or inscribed

steppe: a huge, high semi-arid plain covered with grass

---

aside time for students to share their responses. Don't forget to write thank-you notes to the veterans!

STORY PICTURES: The Assyrians developed the picture tale, which was a series of pictures carved on square stone stelae that told a story, usually of a battle, with captions underneath. The pictures would start at the top of a stela and run down. Let students create their own picture tales by drawing boxes to form a cartoon strip that runs vertically rather than horizontally. They may illustrate a historical event or incidents in their own lives.

CUNEIFORM: Show examples of cuneiform to students. (The University of Pennsylvania has an informative Web site at www.upenn.edu/museum/Games/cuneiform.html). Whittle a pencil tip into a wedge shape. Encourage students to take turns pressing it into a piece of thick, soft clay to produce their own cuneiform writing.

References
*Contenau, Georges. *Everyday Life in Babylon and Assyria.* London: Edward Arnold LTD, 1959.

*Durant, Will. *Our Oriental Heritage.* New York: Simon and Schuster, 1954.

BOOKS FOR STUDENTS

*Landau, Elaine. *The Assyrians.* Brookfield, CT: The Millbrook Press, 1997.

Leon, Vicki. *Outrageous Women of Ancient Times.* Hoboken, NJ: John Wiley & Sons, 1997.

Moss, Carol. *Science in Ancient Mesopotamia.* New York: Franklin Watts, 1999.

*Nardo, Don. *The Assyrian Empire.* San Diego: World History Series, Lucent Books, Inc, 1998.

Oakes, Lorna, and Dr. John Haywood. *Find Out About Mesopotamia: What Life Was Like in Ancient Sumer, Babylon and Assyria.* London: Southwater Publishing, 2004.

*out of print

Greece, 436 B.C.

IN THE GYMNASIUM

CAST OF CHARACTERS

ALEXANDROS, *an athlete from Athens*

CRYSANTHE, *Alexandros's wife*

SIMONIDES, *an athlete from Sparta*

ATEA, *Simonides's wife*

PRIEST

ANNOUNCER

SPECTATORS 1–3

MYRON, *Alexandros's slave*

NARRATORS 1 and 2

SCENE ONE

NARRATOR 1: The year is 436 B.C. Ancient Greece is made up of many city-states. Two of the most powerful city-states, Athens and Sparta, have founded their own colonies and trading posts around the Mediterranean.

NARRATOR 2: Although the city-states share a common language, Athens and Sparta are very different in other ways.

NARRATOR 1: Let's join the athlete, Alexandros, at his home in Athens.

ALEXANDROS: Crysanthe, I'm home! Where are you?

(Crysanthe enters.)

CRYSANTHE: I was in the back rooms weaving, as usual. Tell me—what's going on in the marketplace? Who did you see? I'd love to be able to go there myself—just once.

ALEXANDROS: You can't do that, and you know it.

CRYSANTHE: Don't worry, Alexandros. I know my role as a proper Athenian wife.

ALEXANDROS: When is the *pedagogus* bringing the boys back from school? That slave had better not bring them back late today.

CRYSANTHE: You have an odd look on your face. What's the matter?

ALEXANDROS: I've got some news. I'm going to compete in the Olympic games.

CRYSANTHE: That's wonderful! You're sure to win the one- and four-stade races.

ALEXANDROS: I don't know . . . there's a new runner, Milos from Megara. He's supposed to be fast. What if I lose?

CRYSANTHE: Even if you do, you'll still be honored for all the races you've already won. Then you'll go to work in your father's business. You'll be a good Athenian citizen. And as you say, Athens is the best *polis* in the world.

ALEXANDROS: I want to win. I want to beat Milos more than anything.

CRYSANTHE: I wish I could see you run—just once.

ALEXANDROS: It would be unseemly for a woman to see a field of naked runners!

CRYSANTHE *(sighing)*: I know.

ALEXANDROS: You're not sorry you rode the chariot to my home, are you?

CRYSANTHE: No, of course not. I would marry you all over again. I ate the figs you gave me on our wedding day.

Read-Aloud Plays: Ancient World • Scholastic Teaching Resources

ALEXANDROS: A husband must show his wife that he will provide her with food. It's not her father's responsibility anymore.

CRYSANTHE: And you have kept your promise, Alexandros. The children and I have never gone hungry, but—

ALEXANDROS: But what?

CRYSANTHE: I am hungry to see the world.

SCENE TWO

NARRATOR 2: Meanwhile, in Sparta, Simonides leaves the military barracks where he lives. He hurries to visit his wife, Atea, at home.

ATEA: Simonides! What a welcome surprise!

SIMONIDES: I'm going to the Olympics!

ATEA: I knew you would be selected. What an honor!

SIMONIDES: I love the competition, and seeing athletes from all over Greece. The other city-states have such strange customs.

ATEA: Don't forget you're a Spartan. Don't pay any attention to their crazy views.

SIMONIDES: They all wish they lived here in Sparta.

ATEA: Have you seen our son? The house is so quiet without him!

SIMONIDES: They say our Dameon goes barefoot in the winter without complaining. And he loves his black soup.

ATEA: No one makes black soup as good as mine. You must know exactly how much vinegar and pig's blood to put in it.

SIMONIDES: I can't believe Dameon is seven years old already. Soon enough, he'll find a woman to wrestle and throw over his shoulder. Then he'll be a married man. When he's thirty years old, he'll move out of the barracks to be with her.

ATEA: In only four years, you'll be moving home yourself. I can't wait! Oh, I wanted to tell you: We're making huge profits on our olive oil this year.

SIMONIDES: Excellent! How would we Spartan men be able to prepare for battles if we didn't have strong women like you to take care of business?

ATEA: You must hurry and tell Dameon that you're going to the Olympics. But tell him not to brag. The other boys will be jealous and beat him up.

SIMONIDES: He can take a beating. Did he cry and try to cling to my *chiton* when it was time for him to move into the barracks?

ATEA: No—our Dameon is a true Spartan!

SCENE THREE

NARRATOR 1: A few months later, Alexandros and Simonides travel to Olympia, Greece, to compete in the Olympic Games.

NARRATOR 2: Let's join the athletes at the opening ceremony.

PRIEST: Athletes, you are here not to win games for your own pride and that of your cities, but to do honor to the gods.

ATHLETES: We know it.

PRIEST: Do you swear upon these slices of boar that you will not sin against the Olympic games?

ATHLETES: We swear it.

SCENE FOUR

NARRATOR 1: Let's take a seat in the stands. Alexandros is about to run in his first race, the one-stade race. A stade is one lap around the stadium. The athletes line up and wait for the announcer to begin the race.

ANNOUNCER: On your mark. Get set. GO!

SPECTATOR 1: They're rounding the first turn! Alexandros from Athens is sure to win!

SPECTATOR 2: I'm rooting for the new guy, Milos from Megara. Everybody's talking about how fast he is. Look! Here comes Milos!

ANNOUNCER: At the halfway mark, Alexandros and Milos are neck and neck!

SPECTATOR 3: Milos is really pouring it on! Go, Milos! Go!

SPECTATOR 1: Alexandros can come from behind. I know he can! Come on, Alexandros!

ANNOUNCER: And they're rounding the final turn. Here comes Alexandros! Will he be able to overtake Milos?

SPECTATOR 2: No way!

SPECTATOR 3: Milos just increased his lead!

ANNOUNCER: And the winner is Milos from Megara! But Alexandros came in a very close second! Congratulations!

SCENE FIVE

NARRATOR 2: A dejected Alexandros limps back to the sweat room after the race. Simonides is there, preparing for his wrestling match.

ALEXANDROS: Myron! Bring me a fresh *strigil*. By Zeus, I'm sweaty!

SIMONIDES: You look glum, my friend. Where's your crown of laurel?

ALEXANDROS: Someone else is wearing it.

SIMONIDES: The famous Athenian, Alexandros, was beaten?

ALEXANDROS: Obviously.

SIMONIDES: I watched your race. You're not bad—for an Athenian. But that Milos really snuck up on you.

ALEXANDROS: I *was* there.

SIMONIDES: There's no need to get snappy. Look—we're both Greeks. Not many Athenians come to Sparta. I've always heard wild stories about you all. I'd love to know what Athens is really like.

ALEXANDROS: You're from Sparta, huh? Talk about wild stories—

SIMONIDES: You're getting snappy again. Let's start over again. I'm Simonides. My event is the *pankratium*.

(Myron enters, carrying a towel and a knife.)

MYRON: Master, here's a hot towel and a *strigil*.

ALEXANDROS: Thank you, Myron.

(Myron leaves.)

SIMONIDES: Why did you thank him?

ALEXANDROS: It's the Athenian way.

SIMONIDES: Is he as smart as he looks?

ALEXANDROS: Yes. Why?

SIMONIDES: I'd have him killed.

ALEXANDROS: That's ridiculous.

SIMONIDES: Watch out, or he'll become your master. We Spartans don't want slaves— or *helots*, as we call them—taking over. Our secret police, the Krypteia, spies on them. If we catch a *helot* out at night, we kill him. In fact, killing a helot is part of our training.

Read-Aloud Plays: Ancient World • Scholastic Teaching Resources

ALEXANDROS: I hear your slaves hate you so much they'd eat you raw if they could.

SIMONIDES: At least we Spartans treat our women well. You keep your wives and daughters hidden away indoors.

ALEXANDROS: They stay at home because that's where they'll be safe.

SIMONIDES: One time, a visitor from another city-state was teasing my sister. He said, "You Spartan women are the only ones who can rule men." She replied, "That's because we're the ones who give birth to men." My sister had to learn how to wrestle, throw a javelin, and do gymnastic exercises just as I did.

ALEXANDROS: Whatever for?

SIMONIDES: She had to be strong so she could pass her citizenship test. Then the state could assign her a good husband.

ALEXANDROS: I wouldn't want to live with some spear-throwing Amazon.

SIMONIDES: Spartan men don't live with their wives until after they're thirty. Our wives take care of business while we keep up our military training.

ALEXANDROS: If you're not home, and your wives are so busy, who brings up the children?

SIMONIDES: When we're seven, we leave our mothers and move into barracks. My son is there now.

ALEXANDROS: That's cruel. I'd never give up my children like that.

SIMONIDES: We're taught to survive, even in the wild. Sometimes, we have whipping contests just to see how much pain we can stand.

ALEXANDROS: That's your education? What about learning to read and write?

SIMONIDES: We learn the basics. But if you can't fight and survive, what's the point of knowing how to read and write?

ALEXANDROS: My sons study reading, writing, arithmetic, grammar, and music. *And* they can wrestle and do gymnastics. If they don't do well, their teachers poke them with sticks and tell them that a healthy body leads to a healthy mind.

SIMONIDES: Do you know what my mother said to me when I was a boy? "Come back *with* your shield, or *on* it." It's more important to die an honorable death than to live as a coward.

ALEXANDROS: We Athenians believe you can have it all: freedom and discipline, ideas and action, ambition and energy.

SIMONIDES: With ideas like that, you'll never be as tough as we are. But you know what? I kind of like you. Let me tell you a story that will help you win your next race.

Read-Aloud Plays: Ancient World • Scholastic Teaching Resources

ALEXANDROS: I don't need a—

SIMONIDES: There was a Spartan boy in training who had caught a fox. He was about to kill the fox and eat it when some soldiers came along. The boy knew they'd steal the fox and beat him for being unsuccessful. You know what he did?

ALEXANDROS: I'm afraid to ask.

SIMONIDES: The boy stuffed the wild fox under his clothes. The fox bit him in the stomach, but the boy didn't even cry out. He just kept looking casual in front of the soldiers—until he suddenly keeled over. Dead.

ALEXANDROS: What a waste!

SIMONIDES: No, he had the courage to do what he had to do. If a Spartan boy can be that tough, can't an Athenian man?

ALEXANDROS: Your story *has* helped me, Simonides. I'm going to go out there and run faster than I've run before to bring glory to Athens. It truly is the greatest city-state of all.

SIMONIDES: The second greatest city-state.

ALEXANDROS: Simonides, you may be annoying, but we're both Greeks. Think of what would happen if we didn't stick together. The Persians would take over Greece for sure. And if Athens and Sparta ever fought each other, Greece would be lost.

SIMONIDES: No. Sparta would win, and Greece would be stronger than ever.

SCENE SIX

NARRATOR 1: The competitors, including Alexandros and Milos, line up for the four-stade race.

NARRATOR 2: Simonides joins the other spectators in the stands.

ANNOUNCER: On your mark. Get set. GO!

SPECTATOR 1: Oh, no! Alexandros is running too fast. He's never going to be able to keep up that pace!

SPECTATOR 2: Milos is going to wait till Alexandros gets tired, and then he'll fly past the Athenian.

ANNOUNCER: After two stades, Alexandros from Athens remains in the lead. Here comes Milos!

SPECTATOR 1: Alexandros will never last.

SIMONIDES: I wouldn't count him out yet.

SPECTATOR 2: Are you kidding? Look!

ANNOUNCER: And Milos takes the lead at the three-stade mark!

SPECTATOR 3: It looks as if Alexandros is finished. Again.

SIMONIDES: Remember the fox, Alexandros!

SPECTATOR 1: Remember the fox? What's he talking about?

SPECTATOR 2: Who knows? He's a Spartan.

SPECTATOR 3: I don't believe it!

ANNOUNCER: Alexandros is catching up to Milos! He's passing Milos! Alexandros is ahead by two strides! Alexandros is the winner!

SPECTATOR 1: Yea, Alexandros!

SPECTATOR 2: Alexandros is the fastest runner in the world!

SIMONIDES: Excuse me, he's the fastest runner from Athens.

Background on Ancient Greece

People have lived in the beautiful but harsh land of Greece for thousands of years. The ancient Greeks were a single people, but they didn't have a single ruler. Instead, Greece was run as a loosely united group of city-states (or *poleis*). Especially after 800 B.C., these city-states began to grow stronger through trade and by developing their own industries such as making wine and olive oil, fine pottery, and metalworking.

Of the Greek city-states, Athens and Sparta differed the most from each other. Athens was the most sophisticated and important city in Greece. Athenians focused on creative pursuits, the life of the mind, and the development of trade. They also wanted to spread their ideas, particularly the idea of democracy, to other parts of Greece.

The Spartans lived on the large Peloponnesian peninsula south of Athens in a region called Laconia. Their focus was on military discipline and self-defense to an extreme rarely seen in history. Sparta led the Peloponnesian League, a group of city-states including Megara, Corinth, and Argos that banded together for self-defense.

The Golden Age

This play is set during Athens's Golden Age. During this 50-year period, which began with the defeat of the Persians in 479 B.C., Athenian civilization reached its height. Under the leadership of Pericles, Athens underwent a massive building project that included the Parthenon and the temple of Athene Nike, and other buildings in the Acropolis (literally, high place of the city). There was an incredible outpouring of creativity: Artists such as Pheidias made beautiful sculptures, mathematicians such as Pythagoras wrote theorems we still use today, and playwrights such as Sophocles and Euripides wrote some of the greatest plays of all time. Thinkers called sophists began teaching in the marketplace. One of the most famous was Socrates, who taught Plato, who would later teach Aristotle—a chain of three great philosophers.

Greek Against Greek

Tensions grew between Athens and Sparta and erupted into a bitter civil war; the Peloponnesian War was fought between 431 and 404 B.C. The Spartan victory was helped by a plague that hit Athens. Eventually, however, Sparta's dominance faltered when the city-state of Thebes rose up and defeated Sparta. The Greeks would learn a sad lesson when they lost the unity among the city-states. As they fought each other, they accepted the help of the Romans. Greece was later absorbed into the Roman Empire. The Romans thought the Greeks were cultured and sophisticated but unable to govern themselves. Many Greeks became slaves and pedagogues for Roman children.

The Olympics

The first Olympics took place in Olympia, Greece, in 776 B.C. The games were held to honor Zeus, the king of the gods. In the beginning, the Olympics consisted of only one footrace but later included many events. The games had a deep religious significance to the Greeks, who believed in the power of the body. These religious ceremonies were so important to the Greek city-states that they would even halt wars to hold the games. Although the games were held in several other locations, Olympia was the most important. Only men were allowed to attend the games because the athletes were naked.

Read-Aloud Plays: Ancient World • Scholastic Teaching Resources

Thinking and Discussing

ORDER OR FREEDOM?: The Greeks highly valued freedom and individual choice.

The city-states were successful when they were united, but failed when they fought each other. Talk about the pros and cons of many people or groups working independently; for example, this independence can cause chaos and disorganization but it can also lead to great creativity. Extend the discussion to the role of working independently in the classroom. When is working independently in the classroom most effective and when is it least effective?

THE SPARTAN EXAMPLE: Long ago, the historian Xenophon (ZEH-nuh-fuhn) wrote the following about Sparta: "The most extraordinary thing of all is that despite the universal praise for [Sparta's society], not a single city is willing to copy it." Why would cities be reluctant to follow the Spartan example? Ask students to give examples of Spartan life they think deserve praise.

WOMEN'S WORK: In the play, Crysanthe is relegated to staying at home and working, while the Spartan woman, Atea, runs a business. What might have caused the roles of men, women, and children to evolve differently in Athens and Sparta? Based on the descriptions of children's lives in the play, which city-state, Athens or Sparta, would boys and girls have preferred to live in? Why?

Researching and Doing

HOLD AN ANCIENT OLYMPICS: Hold your own Olympic foot races. Ask students to measure a one-stade racecourse on the school grounds. (One stade is about 200 meters.) Racers may opt to participate in a one-, two-, or four-stade race. Have

---

Vocabulary

chiton: a short tunic worn by Greek men

helot: a Spartan slave

Krypteia: Spartan secret police

pankratium: a sport that was a mixture of boxing and wrestling

pedagogus: a slave whose responsibility is to look after a Greek child's education

strigil: a curved, dull-bladed knife used for wiping off sweat

Zeus: chief god of the Greeks

---

students make laurel crowns out of construction paper for the winners.

GREEK ROOTS: Many words in the English language have Greek origins. Ask students if they can figure out the English translations of the following Greek words: *schole* (school), *philosophia* (philosophy), *demokratia* (democracy), *komoidia* (comedy), *poietes* (poet), *stadion* (stadium), and *athletes* (athlete). Display a dictionary, and look up the words above. Show students how to find the origin of the word. Then divide your class into groups and give each group a dictionary. Time groups to see how many words of Greek origin they can find in fifteen minutes.

GREAT GREEKS: Ask students to research famous Greek leaders, philosophers, artists, and others whose lives continue to affect us today. Here are a few suggestions: Aeschylus, Alexander, Aristides the Just, Aristotle, Aspasia, Cimon, Cleisthenes, Euripides, Homer, Leonidas, Lycurgus, Pericles, Phidias, Socrates, Solon, Theseus, and Thucydides.

THE CORINTHIAN LETTER: Before the Peloponnesian War, the Corinthians sent a letter to their allies, the

---

Spartans, warning them about what Athenians were like. Copy the following excerpt to share and discuss with students:

"And you have never considered what manner of men are these Athenians . . . They are revolutionary, . . . while you are conservative. They are bold beyond their strength; . . . Whereas it is your nature, though strong, to act feebly; . . . they hope to gain something by leaving their homes; but you are afraid that any new enterprise may imperil what you have already. When conquerors, they pursue their victory to the utmost; when defeated, they fall back the least. Their bodies they devote to their country as though they belonged to other men; their true self is their mind . . . If a man should say of them that they were born neither to have peace themselves nor to allow peace to other men, he would simply speak the truth."

Then ask students what they think people in other parts of the world think of the United States. Guide them in researching articles by foreign journalists about America in print or on the Internet. Challenge them to write an opinion piece declaring whether they agree or disagree with the article.

References

*de Camp, L. Sprague. *Great Cities of the Ancient World.* New York: Dorset Press, 1972.

Durant, Will. *The Life of Greece.* New York: Simon and Schuster, 1966.

BOOKS FOR STUDENTS

*Nardo, Don. *Life in Ancient Athens.* San Diego: Lucent Books, 2000.

Oxlade, Chris, and David Ballheimer. *Eyewitness Books: Olympics.* Random House, 1999.

Powell, Anton, and Sean Sheehan. *Ancient Greece, Revisid Edition.* New York: Facts on File, 2003.

out of print

Read-Aloud Plays: Ancient World • Scholastic Teaching Resources

Kush, 24 A.D.

First Day in the Palace

CAST OF CHARACTERS

RAMOSES, *an Egyptian merchant*

ARSINOE, *Ramoses's daughter*

VILLAGER • RAIDERS 1 and 2 • SLAVE TRADER

PAESE, *an enslaved girl, originally of the Blemmyes people*

GOVERNMENT MINISTER

KANDAKE AMANIRENAS, *Queen of Kush*

AKINIDAD, *Amanirenas's son*

GAIUS PETRONIUS, *Roman governor of Egypt*

ENVOY

NARRATORS 1 and 2

Read-Aloud Plays: Ancient World • Scholastic Teaching Resources

SCENE ONE

NARRATOR 1: The year is 24 A.D. Arsinoe and her father Ramoses have stopped at a village to sell their wares. They travel up and down Egypt's Upper Nile River to trade fine linen, glass, and other goods. Many of their customers come from the kingdom of Kush, which is Egypt's southern neighbor.

RAMOSES: It's getting dark, Arsinoe. We should start packing up.

(The Villager enters.)

ARSINOE: After this customer, Father. *(to the Villager)* Please, feel the linen. It's perfect for clothes or for wrapping mummies.

VILLAGER: That *is* nice. Let me have ten yards.

(The Villager pays for the fabric and leaves.)

RAMOSES: You're a natural-born merchant, Arsinoe. Look at all this gold. We've make a fine profit here.

ARSINOE: You're a good teacher, Dad. I learned it all from you.

RAMOSES: This is a strange life for a young girl, traveling up and down the river, selling things, instead of living in a nice mud-brick house with neighbors around. I hope your Mama thinks I'm doing the wise thing.

ARSINOE: She would want us to be together. I know that.

(Raiders 1 and 2 enter. They stay at the edge of the marketplace, watching Ramoses and Arsinoe and their goods.)

RAIDER 1: Look at that ship full of goods. Let's steal it.

RAIDER 2: Let's take the man and girl, too. We can sell them in Kush.

(The Raiders ambush Ramoses and Arsinoe.)

RAIDER 1: Get your hands up!

RAMOSES: Please—take the boat, but leave us alone!

RAIDER 2: Are you kidding? We can get good money for you—especially for your daughter. She looks young and strong.

RAMOSES: You're not turning my daughter into a slave!

RAIDER 1: Be quiet, or we'll dump you into the river. You'll be crocodile chow.

ARSINOE: Don't touch my father!

RAIDER 2: Pipe down, or he goes overboard.

Read-Aloud Plays: Ancient World • Scholastic Teaching Resources

SCENE TWO

NARRATOR 2: The raiders sell Arsinoe and her father to a slave trader going to Meroë (Mer-O-ee), the capital of Kush. As the traders march their captives south, they travel through harsh desert. Then they pass grasslands where people are herding cattle. Approaching Meroë, they see large fields of barley. Animal-powered water wheels pump water into irrigated ditches and woodlands. Suddenly, Arsinoe sees a strange-looking mountain.

ARSINOE: That's the strangest mountain I've ever seen.

RAMOSES: That's a slag heap. It's where they put the material left over from making iron. You can see the iron mine over there.

SLAVE TRADER: Egypt doesn't have iron ore like Kush does. Slaves work in our mines, digging out the ore to make into iron to make into weapons. They don't last long in the mines. You'd better hope you don't get sold to work there.

(Ramoses waits to speak until the Slave Trader has left.)

RAMOSES: Arsinoe, they're going to sell us in the slave market. And they aren't going to sell us together.

ARSINOE: I can't be separated from you!

RAMOSES: Dry your tears. Look strong and confident. You have the best chance to be sold into a desirable position. Shhh!

(The Slave Trader returns.)

SLAVE TRADER *(to Arsinoe)*: You know the languages of Kush, the Romans, and the Egyptians. You're strong and fit, too. I bet the palace will take you.

ARSINOE: What about my father? He's well educated, too.

SLAVE TRADER: If he's so smart, he'd tell you to keep quiet.

SCENE THREE

NARRATOR 1: Arsinoe becomes a slave in the royal palace of Meroë. Ramoses is separated from his daughter at the slave auction. Arsinoe has no idea where her father has been taken. One day, she and another enslaved girl, Paese, are ordered to kill flies in the palace with giraffe's tail flyswatters.

PAESE: You hold the swatter like this and—got one!

ARSINOE: I missed.

PAESE: Try again. It's all in the flick of the wrist.

ARSINOE: Thanks for helping me. It feels so strange to be here.

PAESE: I remember that feeling.

ARSINOE: How long have you been here?

PAESE: Since I was seven. You're from Egypt, aren't you?

ARSINOE: Yes. How could you tell?

PAESE: You look Egyptian. There are tons of Egyptians here in Kush who've fled from the troubles in your country. They gather in restaurants and cry into their bowls of barley about the good old days.

ARSINOE: In a strange way, Kush is a lot like home.

PAESE: It should be, considering it was in Egypt's shadow for thousands of years.

ARSINOE: What happened to you? Why are you a slave in your own country?

PAESE: I'm not a Kushite. Many different people live in the vast savannahs around Kush. My people are the Blemmyes. We grazed herds of cattle in the grasslands east of Meroë. When we were thirsty, we drank our cows' milk or gave them a cut and drank their blood. When we were hungry, we ate cheese made from their cream. Then our cattle got sick and died. My family had to sell me into slavery to pay the bills. I'm lucky to be in the palace.

ARSINOE: I don't feel lucky to be here!

PAESE: Believe me, we *are* lucky. We get enough barley, millet, and cheese to eat, decent clothes to wear, and a safe place to sleep. Besides, there are so many slaves here that we don't have to work very hard. Living in the palace has other benefits, too.

ARSINOE: Like what?

PAESE: Hardly anybody notices us, but we can notice everything. It's like being a part of history. For example—bow down on the floor! Quick!

(Arsinoe and Paese bow. Kandake Amanirenas passes by them. They rise after she leaves.)

PAESE: That was the Kandake! The queen!

ARSINOE: The queen?

PAESE: Yes. The best queen in the world!

ARSINOE: Amanirenas isn't even the queen of your people! She's enslaved you and you call her *your* queen?

PAESE: Kandake Amanirenas is tough. I like that. You'll grow to admire her, too.

ARSINOE: Our Queen Cleopatra was the best queen.

PAESE: Why do you think so well of her?

Read-Aloud Plays: Ancient World • Scholastic Teaching Resources

ARSINOE: Cleopatra kept the Romans from taking over Egypt for as long as she lived. She and the Roman leader Marc Antony stood together and fought the Romans and almost beat them, too. She lost the gamble—but she was tough! And she was slim and beautiful—

PAESE: *Slim* and beautiful? Who wants a scrawny queen? We like our queens to have some meat on them. What's the point of being rich if you look like you don't have enough food to eat?

ARSINOE: Speaking of food, I'm starving. I'd give anything to have a bowl of dates right now.

PAESE: You'd better keep your mind on swatting flies.

SCENE FOUR

NARRATOR 2: In the next year, Arsinoe and Paese travel to different parts of the empire as they serve the queen. They go to the lion temples where they see live lions in cages. At Napata, the ancient capital of Kush, the girls see the tall, narrow pyramids of kings and queens. They visit the grounds where war elephants are trained to fight in battles. Then, one afternoon, while Arsinoe and Paese are fanning Kandake Amanirenas with palm fronds, a government minister arrives with news.

MINISTER: Your Majesty, the Roman governor, Gaius Petronius, is leaving his head-quarters in Elephantine, Egypt, to put down a rebellion in Arabia.

KANDAKE: Then this is the perfect time to attack the Romans. They can't force us to pay them taxes because they captured Egypt.

MINISTER: They are extremely greedy.

KANDAKE: They don't like us raiding Egypt's borders. That's too bad.

MINISTER: The Romans *might* be good for trade—

KANDAKE: *I'll* decide whether to do business with the Romans or not—after I defeat them. Summon my son Akinidad and my generals.

SCENE FIVE

NARRATOR 1: The queen and her son lead an attack against a Roman fort across the Egyptian border. Although the Kushites win the battle, it was at a cost to the queen.

PAESE: It's true! I heard Akinidad say that the Kandake has lost the sight in one eye!

ARSINOE: I have to admit that she's a brave woman. She was out there in front, leading the soldiers.

PAESE: The Kandake would never ask a soldier to do something she wouldn't do herself.

ARSINOE: She's lucky she was only wounded and not killed.

PAESE: Quick! Bow down!

(Kandake Amanirenas, with a bandage over one eye, enters. She walks up to a statue of the Roman Emperor Augustus Caesar.)

AMANIRENAS: My people will never pay taxes to you, Augustus Caesar. Akinidad! Bring your sword!

(Akinidad enters, carrying a sword.)

AKINIDAD: What is it, Mother? Have the Romans returned?

AMANIRENAS: Cut off the statue's head. I want to send a message to the Romans. This is what I'll do to the real emperor if he tries to rule Kush!

AKINIDAD: I'll throw the head into the Nile and—

AMANIRENAS: No. We're taking the emperor's head back to Kush with us. I'm going to bury it. The Romans will never find it.

SCENE SIX

NARRATOR 2: The Romans never do find the statue's head. But a few days later, Roman soldiers led by Gaius Petronius recapture the fort. Amanirenas and the Kushite soldiers retreat into Kush. Then both sides agree to a three-day truce— which is soon broken. Kandake Amanirenas and her troops face the Romans at the Kushite city of Primis. The Romans win the battle and go on to burn the ancient Kush capital, Napata.

NARRATOR 1: There is a discussion in the Roman camp.

GAIUS PETRONIUS: I know Amanirenas well. That one-eyed queen will never give up—no matter how many battles she loses.

ENVOY: I've never seen such a fierce fighter. Perhaps it would be better to make peace with her.

GAIUS PETRONIUS: Find out what she wants. But tell her that we want the head of Augustus Caesar back!

ENVOY: Yes, Governor.

SCENE SEVEN

NARRATOR 2: Meanwhile, in the Kush camp. . . .

ENVOY: Why should we fight each other when we can help each other?

AMANIRENAS: You mean when you can help yourself to Kush's riches.

ENVOY: Your kingdom *is* rich, Your Majesty. Rome only asks for a small amount of money from you. In exchange, we offer you the protection of our army.

AMANIRENAS: What I need—and have—is protection *from* your army. Now let me tell you what I want. Kush will not pay taxes to Rome. What I will do is open up Kush to Roman trade.

ENVOY: The emperor will never agree to that!

AMANIRENAS: Every day, camels come to Meroë from the western desert and the south and east. They bring gems, frankincense and myrrh, ostrich feathers, leopard skins, wild animals, gold, and slaves. It will be easier for you Romans to do business with us and our trade networks than for you to go to some unfamiliar place deeper in Africa.

ENVOY: You do make a good point. Kush is a long way from Rome. You could make Africa's riches accessible to us. Very well, I'll take your suggestions to the emperor.

AMANIRENAS: They're not suggestions. They're demands which must be met.

ENVOY: There is one other thing—the matter of the emperor's head?

AMANIRENAS: If you can find it, you can have it back.

SCENE EIGHT

NARRATOR 1: Kush and Rome sign a treaty. Trade between the two empires is opened. Kush will no longer have to pay taxes to Rome. Although the Kandake will break the treaty in a few years, life at the palace returns to normal.

ARSINOE: I can't believe I'm saying this, but it's good to be back at the palace.

PAESE: It was so exciting seeing our Kandake fight the Romans and then make peace with them.

ARSINOE: She's so tough. I couldn't believe it when she told Akinidad to cut off that statue's head.

PAESE: The Romans will never find it!

ARSINOE: They'd never dare to dig up the floor of a Kushite temple.

PAESE: I bet that head's going to be buried there forever.

NARRATOR 2: The bronze head was found in the 1800s. Today, it can be seen at the British Museum in London.

Read-Aloud Plays: Ancient World • Scholastic Teaching Resources

Background on Kush

The kingdom of Kush (also known as Nubia) was one of the greatest of Africa's ancient kingdoms. Located in what is now Sudan, Kush's history was closely intertwined with Egypt's. Kushite soldiers were considered the backbone of Egypt's army, and many Kushite leaders became high-ranking officials in the Egyptian government. Egypt relied on Kush for its valuable supply of gold and trade routes with central Africa, which provided precious goods. In turn, the Egyptians built temples and shared their culture and gods with Kush.

In about 750 B.C., Kush emerged as an independent kingdom. During the 700–600s B.C., the Kushite kings of the twenty-fifth dynasty captured Egypt and became its pharaohs. The original Kush capital city of Napata was close to the fourth cataract of the Nile, but over time, the city of Meroë grew as it gained fame as an iron-smelting center. Both the ore and the wood to burn it could be found near Meroë. Furthermore, the city was 350 miles south, which made it safer from invasion. The Meroitic period lasted from ca. 295 B.C. to A.D. 320.

Some experts believe that Kush eventually fell because so many trees were cut down to smelt their iron. The environment deteriorated because Kushites couldn't grow new trees fast enough; there were no tree roots to hold down the good soil, so rains washed it away. Other civilizations also began to develop—including a people called the X Group, and the kingdom called Axum—that took away trade from Kush. Nomadic groups probably surrounded Kush, eventually attacking and finishing off the kingdom.

Slavery in Ancient Times

Untold millions of people spent their lives trapped in slavery throughout the ancient world. There were many reasons why people were enslaved: Some were prisoners of war, some lost all their money and sold themselves to pay debts, some were kidnapped from their homes. Slavery was a profitable business and an accepted practice in ancient times. It was an important component of Kush's trade, and Kush was one of the ancient world's major slave markets. Wealthy people throughout the ancient world benefited from the free labor of slaves.

Language and Geography

Kush developed its own language and writing. Unfortunately, the language died out. Although we can sound out words, we don't know what they mean. We do know that the landscape has changed. That region of Africa has become much drier and less able to sustain life than it was when the kingdom of Kush was flourishing.

Thinking and Discussing

GOING WITH THE FLOW: Locate the Nile River on a map and explain that it originates in the south. Also point out other major rivers, and discuss how rivers generally originate: they usually start in the mountains and terminate in large bodies of water, most often the sea. Are there rivers near where you live? Where do they begin and end? Let students study maps, globes, and atlases to find large cities that have grown up alongside rivers, such as London, New York, Paris, and Rome. Why do students think these cities are situated where they are? In what ways might a river shape a culture?

ARSINOE'S DILEMMA: Arsinoe's life took an unexpected turn in the play. How would students cope if they were forced to live a life they didn't choose? What strengths would they draw on to make the best of the situation? Discuss how students have coped with difficult events in the past.

DEALING WITH ENEMIES: The people of Kush did business with the Romans even though they were enemies. What are the practical reasons behind doing business with people who are your enemies? Have any students had to work on a project or activity with someone they didn't like or who didn't like them? How did they handle the situation? What are the benefits and drawbacks of taking a businesslike attitude toward your opponents?

Researching and Doing

KUSHITE BOWL: Materials needed include clay, and a pencil or plastic knife.

The people of Kush were famous for their delicate pottery, including vases, bowls, and plates that were decorated either with paintings or incised etchings. Have students shape bowls out of clay and decorate them with patterned designs. They may use pencils or plastic knives to create patterns on the sides of the bowls. Let the bowls dry. Use this activity to talk about why people in an ancient culture (and today) might work to make objects that are functional as well as beautiful.

FLY PIN: Materials needed include cardboard (from a cereal box),

---

Vocabulary

cataract: rapids in a river

frankincense: an aromatic resin used for making perfume

irrigated: dry land that is watered by pipes or ditches

kandake: a queen in Kush

merchant: a person who sells

myrrh: a resin that comes from special Arabian and African trees that is used for incense and for medicine

savannah: a flat grassland in a warm region

truce: a temporary halt in a fight

---

aluminum foil, and tape or pins.

Archaeologists have found many pins that represent flies in the graves of Kushite soldiers. These metal pins were a mark of bravery. The peoples of the Nile believed their soldiers should be as persistent and hardy as flies! Show students how to make their own fly pins. They cut the shape of a fly's wings out of cardboard and then cover them with aluminum foil (and tape, if necessary). Students can use tape or pins to attach the pins to themselves.

AFRICAN KINGDOMS: Kush and Egypt were the earliest kingdoms in Africa, but many other ancient kingdoms rose and fell. Ask students to research other kingdoms, such as Mali, Ghana, Zimbabwe, Ethiopia, Benin, and the Songhai empire. A great resource is the Henry Louis Gates book found in the reading list.

References

*Brooks, Lester. *Great Civilizations of Ancient Africa.* New York: Four Winds Press, 1972.

Burstein, Stanley, ed. *Kush and Axum.* Princeton, NJ: Markus Wiener Publishers, 1998.

Emery, Walter B. *Egypt in Nubia.* London: Hutchinson and Co. Publishers, 1965.

Gates, Henry Louis. *Wonders of the African World.* New York: Alfred A. Knopf, 1999.

*Keating, Rex. *Nubian Rescue.* London: Robert Hale & Company, 1975.

O'Connor, David. *Ancient Nubia: Egypt's Rival in Africa.* Philadelphia: The University Museum of Archaeology and Anthropology, University of Pennsylvania, 1993.

Reader, John. *Africa: A Biography of the Continent.* New York: Vintage Books, 1997.

Snowden, Frank M. Jr. *Blacks in Antiquity.* Cambridge, MA: The Belknap Press of Harvard University Press, 1970.

BOOKS FOR STUDENTS

*Davidson, Basil, and eds. *African Kingdoms.* New York: Great Ages of Man Series, Time-Life Books, 1971.

Haskins, James, and Kathleen Benson. *African Beginnings.* New York: Lothrop, Lee and Shepard, 1998.

Service, Pamela F. *The Ancient African Kingdom of Kush.* Tarrytown, NY: Marshall Cavendish, 1998.

*out of print

Rome, 100 A.D.

AT THE COLOSSEUM

CAST OF CHARACTERS

MARCIA, *a Roman woman*

LIVIA, *a Roman woman*

TERTIA, *a Roman woman*

MARIUS, *a gladiator from Greece*

TAHARQUA, *a gladiator from Kush*

VERCINGETORIX, *a gladiator from Gaul*

ANNOUNCER • SAUSAGE VENDOR

SLAVE MASTER • CHRISTIANS 1–3

ROMANS 1–3

SLAVES 1 and 2 *(nonspeaking roles)*

NARRATORS 1 and 2

Read-Aloud Plays: Ancient World • Scholastic Teaching Resources

SCENE ONE

NARRATOR 1: In the year 100 A.D., the Roman empire is the most powerful empire the world has seen. The Romans have built special theaters called colosseums all across their empire. For entertainment, they watch gladiators, specially trained slaves, fight each other in these colosseums. The Romans believe that seeing bloodshed will make them tough for battle.

NARRATOR 2: Today, two friends—Marcia and Livia—sit high up in the women's section in Rome's Colosseum, waiting for the games to begin.

MARCIA: Tertia's late.

LIVIA: She's never late.

(Tertia rushes in.)

MARCIA: You're late.

LIVIA: You're never late.

TERTIA: There was a *huge* traffic jam: crowds of workers, beggars, toga venders, shoving and pushing. Then some fool threw a plate out of his window and nearly killed one of the slaves carrying my litter!

LIVIA: Thank Jupiter you're all right. Rome gets more and more crowded every day. Donkey carts carrying people grind away all day on the cobblestones. Then the supply wagons rumble all night. It's so stressful.

MARCIA: That's what happens when you have more and more people cramming themselves into the capital city of the world's greatest empire.

TERTIA: The procession's starting! There must be dozens of lions and bears and giraffes marching around the stage.

LIVIA: Here come the chained prisoners. I hear they're Christians.

MARCIA: If they don't want to die, all they have to do is repeat an invocation to the gods and offer incense and wine to a statue of our emperor.

TERTIA: They show no respect for the official gods of the Roman Empire.

LIVIA: The gladiators are coming out. Which one is it that you like, Marcia?

MARCIA: Marius—there he is, way down to the right.

LIVIA: Is he the one they call the Glory of the Girls?

TERTIA: Are you kidding? The one with the broken nose and all the scars?

MARCIA: That means he's tough and manly. He's a Greek, so I'll bet he's intellectual and poetic, too. He's been in at least a dozen contests. Wait till you see him fight.

Read-Aloud Plays: Ancient World • Scholastic Teaching Resources

TERTIA: We'll have to wait for the bears to fight the lions and the prisoners to get chewed up by the lions and—

MARCIA: The boring part.

LIVIA: I thought you liked animals.

MARCIA: It's not the same as watching two skilled gladiators struggle to the death.

TERTIA: These contests are supposed to go on for one hundred twenty-three days, so we'll see plenty of action.

LIVIA: Thousands of animals are going to be killed, and nineteen thousand gladiators will be fighting. Ever since Emperor Trajan defeated the Dacians, he's been spending money like water on entertainment for us.

TERTIA: Remember the triumph when Trajan paraded the prizes and slaves he captured? We're living in wonderful times, aren't we, ladies?

MARCIA: We have a noble emperor on the throne, and Rome is bigger, richer, and stronger than it's ever been.

TERTIA: Do you know what I heard about Emperor Trajan? He visits the homes of ordinary citizens and has dinner with them. He wants to see how his people live.

MARCIA: When Trajan goes on campaigns with the soldiers, he doesn't ride in a litter. He walks like all the other soldiers do.

LIVIA: Ooh! I feel something in my hair.

MARCIA: Let me see, Livia. It's a roasted chickpea. The peasants down there must be throwing food.

TERTIA: I don't understand why they encourage that riffraff to come to Rome—never mind entertaining and feeding them for free. Bread and circuses, that's what's corrupting us.

MARCIA: If the peasants stay in the provinces, they have to work hard and pay taxes. If they come to Rome, they pay no taxes and receive ten pounds of free flour a month *and* free entertainment.

LIVIA: Slaves are doing most of the work around the empire, so there's hardly any work. Small farmers are losing their land to large landowners, so they have nowhere to live. If the emperor tried to stop the bread and circuses, there'd be riots in the street.

MARCIA: Why don't the peasants go to the baths? Trajan's built beautiful temples for bathing, yet it looks—and smells—like they've never been to one.

Read-Aloud Plays: Ancient World • Scholastic Teaching Resources

TERTIA: And it's not as if they're Romans. There are foreigners everywhere you look— a Kushite nobleman on a litter here, Scythians selling broccoli on the street there, a blue-tattooed barbarian from Britain being led off to the slave markets. All of them speaking their own languages or such bad Latin that it hurts my ears.

MARCIA: Except for Marius. He's one foreigner I like.

SCENE TWO

NARRATOR 1: When the procession in the Colosseum ends, the gladiators are forced into cells behind the stage. Marius, Taharqua, and Vercingetorix watch the action onstage and talk to each other as they wait for their turn to fight.

MARIUS: Listen to the roaring of the crowd. These Romans are worse than the cruelest barbarians. How can they make a sport of death?

TAHARQUA: I believe you're Greek? I recognized your accent.

MARIUS: I'm Marius. I was a teacher in Greece. Where are you from?

TAHARQUA: I'm Taharqua from the kingdom of Kush, south of Egypt. I was a trader: furs, elephants, giraffes, gold. The Romans kidnapped me, and here I am.

VERCINGETORIX: I think I'm going to throw up.

TAHARQUA: First time, eh? Where are you from, boy?

VERCINGETORIX: From Gaul. I used to have a farm. I didn't think farm life was so great then, but now—

MARIUS: The Romans think they're so civilized, but do their accomplishments equal those of the Greeks? When we ruled the world, we had slaves and colonies, too. But we were fair and just. Romans get their pleasure from watching people die for sport. They may be brilliant fighters, but where's the poetry in them?

VERCINGETORIX: I don't think I'll be able to kill anyone.

TAHARQUA: Didn't they teach you anything at your *ludi*? Didn't you pay attention at gladiator school?

VERCINGETORIX: They tried to teach us to be mean and to fight. I can't remember anything I learned.

MARIUS: Shhh. Don't let the other gladiators hear you. I see they gave you a trident but no armor so that makes you a *retarius*. The *secutors* have armor and a sword, but not a net like you have. Just remember—swing your net over their heads, yank it till they fall down, and then spear them with your trident.

VERCINGETORIX: I can't do this!

TAHARQUA: It's fight or die, my young friend. You'd better fight.

Read-Aloud Plays: Ancient World • Scholastic Teaching Resources

SCENE THREE

NARRATOR 2: Livia, Marcia, and Tertia talk as a lion kills a giraffe. A vendor wanders through the crowd selling sausage.

SAUSAGE VENDOR: Sausage! Get your fresh sausage here!

TERTIA: Over here! We'll have three sausages. My treat, ladies.

SAUSAGE VENDOR: Thanks for the tip, Madame!

LIVIA: Thank you, friend!

TERTIA: My pleasure.

MARCIA: It's getting hot. I'm sweating into my *stola*.

TERTIA: The wool is so itchy.

MARCIA: Thank goodness they put up the shade. We'd broil in this sun.

LIVIA: It's not fair that the men get the best seats. We sit up high in the back, and they get the seats down in front.

TERTIA: Are you kidding? Roman women are the luckiest women in the world. We're honored as the *materfamilias*. We bear Rome's sons. We're strong enough to raise our children and handle our estates while our husbands are away.

LIVIA: Speaking of husbands, how was your cousin Lucilla's wedding?

TERTIA: Well, her boyfriend Julius is being sent to Gaul as a centurion. We thought they'd have to be married in May.

MARCIA: *May?* What a bad omen that would be: "Wed in May, rue the day!"

TERTIA: True, but Lucilla's fifteen. Too much older, and no one would marry her. Luckily, Julius isn't leaving until July.

LIVIA: Have they gotten married yet?

TERTIA: Yes, and Lucilla looked beautiful—all dressed in white with her hair braided into six locks. She also wore a flame-colored veil with a circlet of herbs on top. Then she dedicated her dolls to our family gods. She had tears in her eyes as she laid down her *bulla*. She's had that amulet since she was born.

MARCIA: Traditions are important. A Roman wedding should be a Roman wedding.

TERTIA: It was a Roman wedding all right. They sacrificed a sheep. The priest cut out its liver, and the omens were good. Since I was the *pronuba,* I told the bride and groom to join hands and repeat their vows to each other.

LIVIA: That's so romantic!

(They all sigh.)

Read-Aloud Plays: Ancient World • Scholastic Teaching Resources

MARCIA: When I got married, I thought I was so grown-up, dedicating my dolls to the household gods.

TERTIA: The best part's the day after the wedding. Then you're a respectable married lady, a *matrona*.

MARCIA: The first day one wears a woman's *stola*!

LIVIA: The slaves do what *you* say, not what your mother says!

MARCIA: And last but not least, one has a husband.

LIVIA: If one's husband is ever around.

MARCIA: Oh, Livia! Haven't you heard from Cassius?

LIVIA: I know my husband's busy guarding the frontier against the Gauls, but I'm getting worried. I haven't heard from him in three months.

MARCIA: I'm sure Cassius is fine.

TERTIA: How's your son Flavius?

LIVIA: He's away, too, studying in Greece. The Greeks may not be able to hold together an empire, but they certainly are cultured. Flavius will have the most important skills a proper young gentleman should have—the ability to give proper speeches.

MARCIA: You must be so proud. I hope that's a comfort until you hear from Cassius.

LIVIA: What would I do without you two? Oh, look—here come the Christians!

SCENE FOUR

NARRATOR 1: In the ring below, the Christians are shoved into the center of the stage by slaves. They huddle in a group and cling to each other. From their cell, the gladiators watch.

ANNOUNCER: This is your last chance. Will you repent and worship the gods of Rome?

CHRISTIANS: NO!

ANNOUNCER: Very well. Unleash the lions.

NARRATOR 2: A grate at the edge of the stage rises. Snarling lions burst into the ring. The Christians scream as the lions attack.

TAHARQUA: Those Christians didn't stand a chance.

Read-Aloud Plays: Ancient World • Scholastic Teaching Resources

VERCINGETORIX: Why didn't they just say they'd worship the Roman gods? I'd say anything to keep from being eaten by lions.

MARIUS: Why don't the Romans let them believe what they want?

TAHARQUA: If people aren't afraid of the Roman gods, they might rebel against the empire. The Romans want everyone to bow to their mighty power.

(The slave master enters the cell.)

SLAVE MASTER: Prepare to fight for your lives. And remember—the emperor paid good money for you. You'd better put on a good show.

MARIUS: What do we care? We're not getting the money!

(The other gladiators laugh but then look serious as they hear the crowd roar.)

TAHARQUA: Good luck to you.

MARIUS: And to you.

VERCINGETORIX: I'm so scared.

MARIUS: Be bold. Fight hard. Pretend you're fighting the Romans. I concentrate all my fury on them. How I'd like to get my hands on some fine upstanding Roman citizen and spear him with my trident!

(The gladiators march into the center of the colosseum.)

SCENE FIVE

NARRATOR 1: After the bodies of the Christians are pulled out of the colosseum, the blood is washed off the stage.

MARCIA: It always takes them so long to wash away the blood. It's so boring. I want to see Marius fight.

TERTIA: The gladiators are coming out!

NARRATOR 2: The gladiators enter the colosseum and stand before the emperor.

LIVIA: It's a shame that most of those magnificent gladiators will die today.

TERTIA: It's better to be a gladiator and die in a blaze of glory than work in a salt mine. Or as a galley slave, rowing a boat until you die of thirst.

MARCIA: They have a chance to earn their freedom if they win enough fights.

Read-Aloud Plays: Ancient World • Scholastic Teaching Resources

NARRATOR 1: The gladiators hold up their swords.

GLADIATORS *(holding up their swords):* We who are about to die salute you.

MARCIA: Look at Marius! He's fighting like a crazy man.

NARRATOR 2: Marius and another gladiator, Octavius, circle each other. Octavius slashes at Marius with his sword but misses.

MARCIA: That was a close call!

NARRATOR 1: Marius stabs his trident into Octavius's arm.

ROMAN 1: More! More! We want blood!

NARRATOR 2: Octavius wheels around and stabs Marius in the leg. Marius falls down. Octavius stands over him and points his sword at Marius's throat. He looks up at the crowd.

MARCIA: Oh no! Get up, Marius! Get up!

ANNOUNCER: Ladies and gentlemen, should Marius be saved or should he die?

MARCIA: Thumbs up! Thumbs up!

ROMAN 2: Kill him! Kill him!

ROMAN 1: Death to Marius!

TERTIA: No! Let him live!

ROMAN 3: Thumbs down!

ANNOUNCER: The crowd's decision is—thumbs down!

NARRATOR 1: Octavius finishes off Marius as the crowd screams in delight.

LIVIA: Here comes the slave dressed like death to drag Marius's body offstage.

TERTIA: What a disappointment! Poor Marcia!

MARCIA: Wasn't that Octavius who killed him? I like the looks of him. They call him Maiden's Delight. Yea, Octavius!

Background on Ancient Rome

The first Romans were farmers who lived in central Italy and then expanded into the rest of Italy. By 100 B.C., Rome had begun to move abroad, annexing Macedonia and conquering Corsica, Spain, Sicily, Sardinia, and northern Africa. At its height, the Roman Empire eventually extended thousands of miles and was governed by a small group of Rome's most powerful families.

Eventually, Rome grew too big. After a long period of political instability, the great military leader, Julius Caesar, was named dictator for life. But many Romans were unhappy that one man had so much power. Caesar was assassinated in 44 B.C. After his death, there was more turmoil. Then, in 27 A.D., Caesar's nephew, Octavian, who called himself Augustus, became Rome's first emperor.

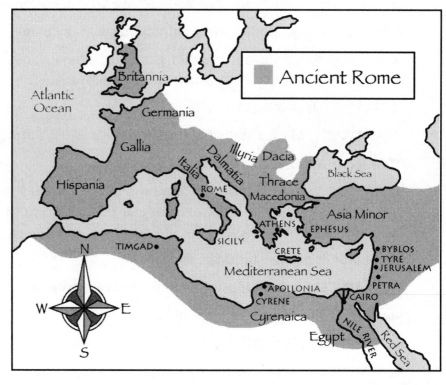

The Imperial Age

Under its emperors, Rome continued to grow. For 200 years, the Roman Empire experienced great stability. This time period is known as the Pax Romana, or Roman peace. The empire controlled lands from northern Africa, west to England, and as far as the Persian Gulf in the east. The Romans put their stamp on everything they conquered. They constructed both aqueducts to carry water and sturdy roads for the transport of soldiers and for goods. They built entirely new settlements, some of which still exist today. They established law and order.

As people were able to trade across thousands of miles, they became more prosperous. Less time was devoted to war and self-defense as regions became part of the Roman empire. The down side was that their own resources were sent to feed the insatiable demands of the city of Rome for food and luxury goods. And the Romans forced millions of people into slavery.

Slow Decline

For many years, Rome had strong, effective emperors, including Trajan. The last of these, the philosophical emperor Marcus Aurelius, controlled the empire at its largest point. But Rome was beginning to rot from within. The empire was no longer as rich as it once was, but the divisions between rich and poor deepened.

The military, once a source of pride, began electing "barracks dictators"—rulers chosen by factions of the army. They were corrupt leaders who were assassinated, one after another. Rome was facing another problem. The barbarians to the north were getting stronger. Rome became less able to defend her borders or feed her people. In 475–476 A.D., the German tribes swept south through Rome. The Roman Empire was destroyed.

Women in Rome

Women in Rome had more freedom than in almost any other ancient culture except for Egypt. Although they couldn't hold public office or vote, they could come and go as they pleased and often wielded great power behind the scenes. Wealthy Roman women cared for their husbands' estates in their husbands' absence. Part of the high respect for women had to do with the image Romans had of family life from the earliest days, when Rome was a farming society and families were the most important social unit.

Read-Aloud Plays: Ancient World • Scholastic Teaching Resources

Thinking and Talking

POPULAR ENTERTAINMENT: The Roman emperors provided free—and violent—entertainment in the colosseum for their subjects. Lead a discussion comparing the gladiatorial contests to contemporary forms of entertainment that students are exposed to. What is their assessment of popular entertainment today—do they consider it to be violent? How would they change what they see, read, or listen to if they could?

ROMAN WEDDINGS: The women in the play describe what a Roman wedding was like. Ask students to talk about the weddings they've attended or heard about. How do weddings today compare to the wedding in the play? Chart their responses on a Venn diagram.

FAITH: Christians were put to death because they wouldn't renounce their god and pledge faith to the Roman gods. Were the Romans justified in trying to convert the Christians? Were the Christians right to refuse? Have students ever been in a situation where they've been forced to make a decision about what they believed?

Researching and Doing

BREAD AND CIRCUS: Trajan presented his people with free food and entertainment to keep them from revolting. Divide the class into small groups, and appoint them as chairpeople of a bread-and-circus event. What kind of food will they serve, and to how many people? What kind of entertainment will they feature, and where will it be presented? Ask them also to consider any potential problems such as traffic congestion, an overflow crowd, and so on. Set aside time for groups to present their plans and to take questions from the rest of the class.

Vocabulary

bread and circuses: the practice of giving the mob free amusement and food in exchange for their compliance in not demanding much from the government

bulla: an amulet given to children at birth to protect them

centurion: an officer in charge of a century, a subdivision of the Roman Legion

Dacians: people who lived in what is now Romania

Gaul: a region in what is now France

gladiators: slaves forced to fight each other to the death for a crowd's amusement

invocation: a prayer

litter: a small covered carriage carried by slaves

ludi: a training school for gladiators

materfamilias: matriarch; the honored mother of a family

pronuba: a married bridesmaid

retarius: a gladiator who carried a net and trident

secutor: a gladiator who wore armor and had a sword

stola: a woman's robe

trident: a forked spear

triumph: a parade where Roman leaders displayed treasures from foreign battles

TRAJAN'S COLUMN: The emperor Trajan had a 125-foot column built out of marble. The column tells the story of how Trajan conquered the Dacians. The story is told in a spiral of 23 blocks with more than 2,500 figures that spiral up the column. After showing photos of Trajan's Column, which still stands in Rome, challenge students to create their own column out of stacked oatmeal containers. They can draw and write the story of a personal triumph on strips of paper, which they can attach to the containers.

AUTOBIOGRAPHY OF A ROMAN: Ask students to research the life of a famous Roman. Encourage them to write a first-person memoir reflecting back on the person's life and accomplishments. Suggest the following Romans to jump-start their research: Augustus, Cato, Claudius, Constantine, Cornelia (mother of the Gracchi), Julius Caesar, Juvenal, Livia, Marc Antony, Marcus Aurelius, Marius, Nero, Ovid, Pliny, Scipio Africanus, Seneca, Sulla, Tiberius, Trajan.

References

*Balsdon, J.P.V.D. *Roman Women, Their History and Habits.* New York: The John Day Company, 1963.

Davis, William Stearns. *A Day in Old Rome.* New York: Biblo and Tannen, 1963.

Hanson-Harding, Alexandra L. *Ancient Rome.* New York: Scholastic Professional Books, Scholastic, Inc, 2000.

Treble, H.A., and K.M. King. *Everyday Life in Rome in the Time of Caesar and Cicero.* Oxford: Clarendon Press, 1930.

BOOKS FOR STUDENTS

Genari, Anita. *Emperors and Gladiators.* New York: Peter Bedrick Books, 2001.

Nardo, Don. *Games of Ancient Rome.* San Diego: Lucent, 2000.

Roberts, Paul C., ed. *Ancient Rome.* New York: The Nature Company Discoveries Library, Time-Life Books, 1997.

*out of print

China, 750 A.D.

Examination Day

CAST OF CHARACTERS

THE CHU FAMILY:

YEE-PING, _the mother_

GONG-WEI, _the father_

SHANG, _the eldest son_

MEI-SU, _the daughter_

LI-HAO, _the youngest son_

NARRATORS 1–5

Read-Aloud Plays: Ancient World • Scholastic Teaching Resources

SCENE ONE

NARRATOR 1: The year is 750 A.D., during the time of the T'ang dynasty. We're in the home of the Chu family in Huangzhou, China. The Chus follow the beliefs of Confucianism.

NARRATOR 2: According to these religious beliefs, family life has a rigid order. The father is responsible for the actions of the entire family. The rest of the family, especially the women, are required to obey his rules. This set of rules is called filial piety.

YEE-PING: I have news about Mei-su. I talked to the astrologer—

GONG-WEI: Are the signs good between Mei-su and young Yu-jing? He's a sheep, and our beautiful daughter was born in the Year of the Rat. It's said that the sheep and the rat soon separate. It would be unfortunate if we couldn't marry our daughter to such a promising man, but there's no point if it will end badly.

YEE-PING: The signs are good, Husband. Our Mei-su will soon be married.

GONG-WEI: It will be a shame to lose her. Raising a daughter is like raising a child for another family.

YEE-PING: I hope her mother-in-law will be kind and won't boss her around.

GONG-WEI: Mei is a good and obedient girl. She knows her duty.

YEE-PING: I remember how it felt to be the new daughter-in-law, always having to wait on your family—not that I regret it. But the life of a young married woman isn't easy. You miss your own parents, and your in-laws often treat you like a slave.

GONG-WEI: Surely coming to live with my family wasn't that bad for you?

YEE-PING: No, your mother was a kind woman.

GONG-WEI: And surely Shang's wife, Jin-yin, has no cause to resent you?

YEE-PING: I treat our daughter-in-law well. Although at times, Jin-yin looks as if she's thinking, *all this will be mine someday*. Her duty isn't always done with a good heart. I'm not saying she won't be good at managing money, or ordering supplies, or doing any of the other tasks she'll be responsible for when Shang becomes head of the household. But I do fear she'll be a demanding mother-in-law one day. I hope our Mei will bear many sons so she'll have power in her new family.

GONG-WEI: Many blessings have come with our old age, Yee-ping.

YEE-PING: Indeed, Husband. Until your honored father died, you weren't considered a legal grown-up. Now our sons must do what you want them to, and their wives must serve me. Speaking of wives, we must think about finding a bride for Li-hao?

GONG-WEI: Let's concentrate on getting our youngest son through the government exams first. If he doesn't pass, we won't be able to arrange a good marriage for him.

SCENE TWO

NARRATOR 3: We're in the men's quarters where the males of the Chu family eat and sleep. When Shang and Li-hao were seven years old, they moved here, away from their mother and sister.

GONG-WEI: Shang, how is your work going?

SHANG: Very well, Father.

GONG-WEI: Li, look at your brother. Only in his early twenties, and he's already a government official.

LI-HAO: Yes, Father.

GONG-WEI: He has made our family proud! *And* he passed his exam with flying colors. By the way, how are your studies going?

LI-HAO: Um, fine, Father.

SHANG: Fine? All you do lately is drift around and sigh.

GONG-WEI: Is this true, Li? The exams are in a few weeks. The government only gives them once every three years. You don't want to miss your chance!

SHANG: Maybe my younger brother doesn't care. Maybe he thinks he can stay here at home and eat your food and do no work. You know what Confucius said, "Hard is the case of him who will stuff himself with food all day, without applying his mind to anything . . . in youth not humble, in manhood doing nothing, and living on to old age—that is to be a pest."

GONG-WEI: That's enough, Shang.

SHANG: Yes, Father.

GONG-WEI: Li, is what Shang saying true?

LI-HAO: I'm not as good at schoolwork as Shang.

GONG-WEI: You haven't been working hard enough. I'm concerned about your attitude.

SHANG: If Li doesn't want to study, maybe he should go work in the fields like a peasant. Let him turn his feet on a waterwheel all day. Or work as a common laborer. He can make bricks. Or maybe he'd like to join the circus. Walk around on stilts! Or—

GONG-WEI: Shang!

LI-HAO: I don't know if being a government official is the right thing for me to do.

GONG-WEI: Of course it is!

LI-HAO: Father, please!

(Li runs out of the room.)

SHANG: How disrespectful! What's the matter with young people these days?

GONG-WEI: Perhaps we're putting too much pressure on Li. This exam will determine what he does for the rest of his life. He was working hard until recently.

SHANG: I could offer him some useful tips on studying. If only he would try as hard as I do, Father, he could—

GONG-WEI: I should have Mei talk to him. I will have your mother talk to Mei.

SCENE THREE

NARRATOR 4: Mei-su hurries to do her mother's bidding. She finds Li, her favorite brother, sitting by the goldfish pond in the central courtyard of their home.

MEI-SU: Mother said you were upset.

LI-HAO: You're the only one who understands me, Sister. I remember the first time I saw you after you were born. You reached out and held on to my finger. How cute you were!

MEI-SU: Why are you so upset?

LI-HAO: Everyone tells me what to do. Father and Mother want me to become a government official like Shang, but I want to be a poet! Listen to this poem I wrote:

> The lonely duck
>
> Paddles by the lotus blossoms,
>
> Without another duck
>
> Nearby.

MEI-SU: Hmmm . . .

LI-HAO: Well, how can I become a good poet when I don't have any time? I don't want to take the stupid exam. I'll never be as good as Shang.

MEI-SU: Don't be so silly. Shang is boring. You just have too many ideas in your head to concentrate.

LI-HAO: I wish I could write poetry and *think*. All I do is study.

MEI-SU: There'll be plenty of time to write poetry when you're older. Now you're young and strong. You don't want to live here, without working, all your life.

LI-HAO: I don't care.

MEI-SU: Of course you do. Have you prayed before the altar of our ancestors?

LI-HAO: Yes, but it didn't do any good.

MEI-SU: You're being impossible. Our ancestors would say: Obey your father and do as he wishes.

LI-HAO: I know that's what I'm *supposed* to do. Why does that feel so wrong?

MEI-SU: Because your heart is heavy with tiredness and fear. You aren't remembering how lucky you are.

LI-HAO: Lucky?

MEI-SU: You're lucky to be a man! I wish I could go traveling wherever I wanted, without being carried around in a litter so no one can see me, or locked away in the women's quarters! If you get a good government position, you'll be able to travel. You could go to the capital city Chang'an—the biggest city in the whole world! You'll get to see wonders like the broad Yellow River or the beautiful Kunlun Mountains. You'll be able to travel on the Silk Road. You might even get to see some of those barbarians—the primitive Europeans traders with their strange colorful hair, rough clothing, and simple language. Think how interesting that would be!

LI-HAO: It's too bad you can't take the exams. You should become a government official, not me.

MEI-SU: That's impossible.

LI-HAO: Why is Father so hard on me?

MEI-SU: Remember that your great-grandfather worked the land. He grew rice and worked hard so his sons could be educated. Father wants you to have a good life.

LI-HAO: Look at T'ao Ch'ien. He worked in an office and then quit to write poetry. He found satisfaction in seeking to balance his life. And what did Chuang-tzu say when he was asked to return to the service of the king? "Better to be a live tortoise dragging your tail in the mud than a dead tortoise, sacred and covered with jewels, in a box in the Emperor's palace."

MEI-SU: What if everyone quit or said no? Part of what makes China great is that many of our smartest people are chosen to work in the government.

LI-HAO: I'll probably end up working for somebody who's not as smart as I am.

MEI-SU: Confucius said—

LI-HAO: Believe me, I know everything Confucius said! I've spent my childhood studying his words so that I'll know them by heart for the exam. I've spent my days grinding ink and endlessly writing Confucius's words with my brush so I can practice for the exam!

MEI-SU: How do you know you wouldn't like working for the government? You might even get to live in the imperial court.

LI-HAO: There are so many taking the examination, and so few are chosen. My chances are one in a thousand.

MEI-SU: How many government positions are open?

LI-HAO: I don't know . . . maybe one hundred fifty thousand or more.

MEI-SU: What kinds of positions are there?

LI-HAO: Oh, all kinds of things. Collecting taxes and storing grain. Making sure people follow the laws, overseeing education in the schools, judging cases, working on big projects like building roads and digging canals. And officials stamp lots of documents with their seals. That's all Shang does—push pieces of paper around his desk.

MEI-SU: If Shang can do it, don't you think you can? Surely you can stamp a document as well as your brother. You can do your job, and think in your free time.

LI-HAO: What if I fail the exam?

MEI-SU: Brother, you must try. If you stay at home, Shang will become the head of the family when father dies. Do you want to depend on him?

LI-HAO: How do you know so much, Sister, when you've never been to school? You're the one with the brains in the family!

MEI-SU: I wish girls could go to school. I'm lucky that Father taught me to read—although I haven't studied the classics as much as you have. And I still have ears to listen. Our parents are beginning to plan my marriage.

LI-HAO: Well, that's exciting, isn't it?

MEI-SU: Every girl looks forward to her wedding day: Wearing a bridal gown, moving to a new house, and meeting her husband for the first time.

LI-HAO: Are you really looking forward to it?

MEI-SU: It will be an interesting change. But I wish I could go on real adventures instead of being locked away in the women's apartments.

LI-HAO: Are you afraid?

MEI-SU: What if my husband lifts up my veil and decides I'm not as good looking as the matchmaker said I was? He could send me back here. What shame and humiliation I would bring on our family!

LI-HAO: No way! You're going to have many sons, Mei.

MEI-SU: Thank you, brother. I hope they'll be as good to their sisters as you are to me.

SCENE FOUR

NARRATOR 5: The day of the exam finally arrives. Mei-su waits anxiously for Li-hao to return home.

LI-HAO: Mei, where are you?

MEI-SU: How was the exam?

LI-HAO: As the poets say, "The drudgery of yesterday is forgotten. Today the prospects are vast and my heart is filled with joy."

MEI-SU: Tell me everything that happened.

LI-HAO: At first, I was afraid that I wouldn't remember anything. Then they caught one student cheating! He had written the answers on a silk scarf and tucked it into his sleeve.

MEI-SU: What will happen to him?

LI-HAO: They'll probably put him to death. Those are the rules.

MEI-SU: Did that upset you?

LI-HAO: It's funny. It made me concentrate. I realized I'd studied hard and knew the answers. Then, when I came out, the streets were full of well-wishers and carriages running through the streets and banners were flying. It was the most beautiful sight, Sister! We won't get the results for a while, but I think I did well.

MEI-SU: So you're not ready to hide away and spend your life writing about lonely ducks on ponds?

LI-HAO: I want to see if they test me for the imperial court. Think of all the sights I'll see!

MEI-SU: You must promise to write to me about everything you see. You must be my eyes and ears in the world.

LI-HAO: I promise.

Read-Aloud Plays: Ancient World • Scholastic Teaching Resources

Background on Ancient China

China is one of the world's oldest civilizations, and its accomplishments stretch across nearly 4,000 years of recorded history. Long before the items were seen in the West, the Chinese invented rag paper, the printing press, and gunpowder. One of the greatest periods in China's incredibly rich history was the T'ang Dynasty (618–903 A.D.). Instead of relying solely on its aristocracy during this time, China took its best and brightest males to work in the government, no matter what their station in life was.

Center of the Universe

One reason that China remained cohesive for so long was its geography. China's rich, fertile land is surrounded by desert to the north and west, the Himalayas to the south, and a vast ocean to the east. As Will Durant says in *Our Oriental Heritage,* "Hemmed in, through most of its history, by the largest ocean, the highest mountains, and one of the most extensive deserts in the world, China enjoyed an isolation that gave her comparative security and permanence, immutability, and stagnation."

While Europe was in the middle of the dark ages, China was flourishing. The Chinese called their land the Middle Kingdom because they considered it to be the center of the world. The capital Chang'an (now Xi'an) was the largest city in the world, and it was surely the most elegant, as the wealthy in silk gowns and luxurious fur coats wandered along the city's beautiful canals.

Despite China's geographic isolation, it had a profound effect on its neighbors (present-day Vietnam,

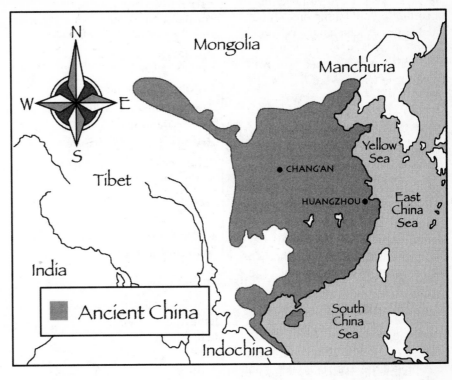

North Korea, and Japan). China also traded goods such as silk and fine porcelain with the West. Medieval explorers Marco Polo and Ibn Battuta traveled to China and were amazed and impressed by what they found.

Religion in China

Ancient China had three strains of religious thought: Taoism, a loosely organized faith, worshiped nature and promoted a simple, balanced life; Buddhism, which came from India, emphasized striving for spiritual transcendence; and Confucianism promoted an orderly world where obedience to family and country were paramount. Although there were sometimes conflicts among these faiths, they managed to coexist and maintain deep roots in Chinese thought.

Thinking and Talking

WOMEN'S LIVES: After reading the play, what can students infer about women's lives and their role in ancient Chinese society? How did people's roles differ inside and outside the family? What kind of life do students think Mei-su will have after she marries?

THE BARBARIANS: Think about Mei-su's attitude toward the barbarians, the Europeans. Compare her attitudes about foreigners with the attitudes of characters in the other plays. How do we as Americans perceive foreigners? Why do we often view people from other countries in an unfavorable light? How do students think people in other countries view us?

FEARING THE FUTURE: Pose the following questions to students:

Examination Day

What attitudes and feelings do you share with the characters in this play, and why? Have you ever felt uncertain before taking an exam or facing another challenge? What did you do to overcome your fears? How have other people helped you overcome these fears? What did that person say or do?

Researching and Doing

DYNASTIES: This play takes place during the T'ang dynasty. At the time of the Assyrian Empire (see "The Old Soldier"), the Zhou dynasty was in power in China. The Qin dynasty and Greece (see "In the Gymnasium") coexisted but probably knew nothing of each other. The Han dynasty ruled China when the Roman Empire (see "At the Colosseum") was in full sway. Ask groups of students to find out more about the Zhou, Qin, Han, and T'ang dynasties. Also instruct them to compare the Assyrian, Greek, and Roman cultures to the corresponding dynasty. To extend this activity, have the class work on an ancient world time line to display.

CHINESE CALLIGRAPHY: Materials needed include tempera paint or a bottle of ink, brushes (preferably with natural bristles), and paper. You will also need sources for Chinese characters such as chineseculture.about.com/library.

Chinese students spend years learning how to form the intricate characters that make up Chinese writing. Show your students a

---

Vocabulary

astrologer: one who studies constellations of stars in the belief that they influence human fates

barbarian: an unflattering term for foreigners

bidding: a command

Confucianism: a belief based on the teachings of Confucius

drudgery: boring, thankless work

filial: relating to or proper for a son or daughter

imperial: relating to an emperor or empire

piety: religious devotion

quarters: living area

Chinese character that has a significant meaning, such as:

fú
(good luck)

shòu
(long life)

Then have them research Chinese calligraphy to find out more about how letters are formed and how writing developed in China. Ask them to illustrate and share their research with the rest of the class.

POETRY READING: Expose students to the magnificent poetry of the T'ang era with a reading of the works of the poets Li Po, Wang Wei, and Tu Fu. Then, encourage them to compose and read their own poetry modeled on T'ang poetry.

CHINESE HOROSCOPE: According to the Chinese calendar, Mei-su was born in the year of the Rat and her intended husband was born in the year of the Sheep. Let students find out which animal sign in the Chinese calendar they were born under and the characteristics of that sign. How well do they feel the sign fits them?

References

Durant, Will. *Our Oriental Heritage*. New York: Simon and Schuster, 1957.

Ebrey, Patricia Buckley. *The Cambridge Illustrated History of China*. New York: Cambridge University Press, 1999.

Goodrich, L. Carrington. *A Short History of the Chinese People*. New York: Harper Brothers Publications, 1943.

BOOKS FOR STUDENTS

Cotterell, Arthur. *Ancient China*. New York: Eyewitness Books, Alfred A. Knopf, 1994.

Fisher, Leonard Everett. *The Great Wall of China*. New York: Aladdin, 1995.

Williams, Suzanne. *Made in China: Ideas and Inventions from Ancient China*. Berkeley: Pacific View Press, 1997.